SURVIVING THE SHARK

SURVIVING THE SHARK

HOW A BRUTAL GREAT WHITE ATTACK TURNED A SURFER INTO A DEDICATED DEFENDER OF SHARKS

By
Jonathan Kathrein and
Margaret Kathrein

With An Introduction
By David McGuire, Director and Founder,
Sea Stewards

And Afterword
By Wallace J. Nichols, PhD

SKYHORSE PUBLISHING

Skyhorse Publishing books may be purchased in bulk at special discounts for sales promotion, corporate gifts, fund-raising, or educational purposes. Special editions can also be created to specifications. For details, contact the Special Sales Department, Skyhorse Publishing, 307 West 36th Street, 11th Floor, New York, NY 10018 or info@skyhorsepublishing.com.

Skyhorse® and Skyhorse Publishing® are registered trademarks of Skyhorse Publishing, Inc.®, a Delaware corporation.

Visit our website at www.skyhorsepublishing.com.

10 9 8 7 6 5 4 3 2 1

Library of Congress Cataloging-in-Publication Data is available on file.

ISBN: 978-1-61608-680-0

Printed in the United States of America

In memory of Mary J. McClellan (1913–2011)
~ mother, grandmother, and great-grandmother ~
who taught us so much and encouraged
us to tell our story.

TABLE OF CONTENTS

ACKNOWLEDGMENTS

Thank you to our family, Reed, Michael, and Eric Kathrein, for supporting us through the shark experience and beyond, and for inspiring us in so many ways, even today.

Thank you to Tricia Fox and Vicky Van Meter for their expert editing and advice.

Credits

We gratefully acknowledge Dr. John McCosker, Senior Scientist and Chair, Aquatic Biology, California Academy of Sciences, for providing information about sharks and shark science.

We gratefully acknowledge David McGuire, Director of Sea Stewards and Research Associate, Department of Aquatic Biology, California Academy of Sciences, for his photographs and contributions on shark science for our chapter "Shark Science."

INTRODUCTION

Sharks loom large in our imagination, and of all sharks, it is the great white shark that looms largest. The media in general and events like the Discovery Channel's "Shark Week" prime our natural atavistic fear with stories of shark attacks and insensible man-eating machines. It is a small wonder that a Midwestern housewife or a schoolchild who has yet to see the ocean fears sharks. Sharks make good press, and white shark attacks make the best press of all.

Living just north of San Francisco, we are in the center of the Red Triangle—the region bounded by Monterey to the south, Point Arenas to the north, and the shark feeding grounds of the Farallones to the west—an area owning the distinction of the greatest number of white shark–human interactions in the world. Whereas most self-preserving surfers and divers avoid coasts posted with shark warnings, as a shark conservationist and documentarian, I seek out sharks and have had many eventful encounters. Yet, among thousands of shark encounters, the closest I have gotten to a shark attack was an ankle nip by a baby blacktip reef shark in a shallow lagoon of the South Pacific. The tiny teeth barely broke through my wetsuit bootee, but we were both surprised. The shark no doubt saw nothing more than a fish-shaped object and was shocked to find it attached to a six-foot human. The speed and the ferocity of this perfectly adapted young shark equally surprised me. Like other sharks, this little shark was just doing what it evolved over millions of years to do. And like its much larger relative, this shark had been equipped with a remarkable sensory and biomechanical tool chest.

It is hard to imagine what it is like to be in the jaws of a three-thousand-pound, sixteen-foot shark, yet in this book Jonathan and his mother Margaret help us to do just that, but in an unexpected, almost tender manner. The fear of a young boy as he is shaken like a rag doll in the maw of a great white is as palpable as a mother's love, and the tragic desperation she must feel for the near loss of one of her children. This is a story of redemption and courage. But what is most remarkable is that this book is a kind of love story, a story of love for the ocean, and, strangely, even for sharks.

Years after his shark experience, I invited Jonathan to speak at a film screening and panel on sharks as part of my non-profit Sea Steward's annual "Sharktober" events. (Sharktober is what surfers call the months when the white sharks reconvene off our shoreline and coincidentally, when the number of human–shark interactions along our coast peaks). A quiet, self-possessed, and handsome young man, Jonathan impressed me as much with his account of the experience as with his motivational appeal. Contrary to the natural response, Jonathan used his experience to discuss the importance of sharks in the ocean, and how we are killing millions more than kill us. With this book, he and his mother have transformed an unimaginably terrifying experience into an allegorical journey of survival, the survival of a species rapidly becoming endangered with extinction. This is a story of "Shark Bites Man, and Man Bites Shark Back" with a ferocity and rapacity heretofore unknown. Consummately adapted to their role as top predators, the hunters have now become the hunted.

As terrible as they may seem, white shark attacks are really very rare, according to white shark expert Dr. John McCosker of the California Academy of Sciences, and in fact most victims, like Jonathan, thankfully survive to tell the story. Yet we are also killing sharks at the rate of tens of millions per year as accidental bycatch on swordfish and tuna longlines, and the shark fin trade supplies an increasing number of fins to satisfy a voracious demand for a luxury soup.

While shark attacks on humans are extremely rare, human attacks on sharks are increasingly common. This loss of sharks is unraveling the tapestry of ocean ecosystems and upsetting the balance in the planet's most important organ. Through our ignorance and even fear, we are erasing the regulators of the sea, the surgeons and the sanitarians that keep fish populations strong, and their habitat healthy and clean. With one-third of oceanic shark species listed as threatened by the International Union for the Conservation of Nature, we are losing sharks before we can even grasp their importance.

We are the apex predators and our consumption is killing not only sharks, but also threatening the entire ecosystem. Once tossed aside as an unwanted commodity, shark fins are increasingly in demand and that demand is creating a brutal black market trade. Sharks are being killed just for their fins, the body cast back into the sea to die, and like the demand for elephant ivory—another unnecessary luxury—people's desire for this coveted appendage has caused shark populations to plummet.

But perhaps we are slowly coming to realize the beauty of sharks and their role in the ocean food web. With stories like this, we are seeing an increase in appreciation that sharks are not just killing machines, but essential components of an integrated ocean ecosystem. Shark sanctuaries are sprouting up in Pacific Island nations like Palau, the Marshall Islands, and the Federated States of Micronesia and other nations like Belize and the Bahamas are following suit. Divers are schooling around sharks, snapping pictures, and as a result, local economies are flourishing.

Countries in South America, Asia, and the EU are increasingly pressured to adopt and enforce sharkfinning laws. Surfers, divers, and ocean activists are shouting out that sharks need protection, and lawmakers are listening. Cities and states are adopting shark fin bans like the one just passed in California. These laws are reducing the flow of and demand for these oceanic blood diamonds. We are taking the fin back and keeping it on the sharks for the ocean and for the future. As our understanding and even love of these misunderstood predators increases, perhaps the media will follow suit and we will continue protecting sharks before it is too late. This story is not another tale of a shark attack; it is a great white shark story of hope.

David McGuire
Director and Founder, Sea Stewards
Research Associate, California Academy of Sciences

SURVIVING THE SHARK

JOURNEY TO
THE COAST

"I learned that life is fragile, and we have to treat
each other well because we don't know when our life,
or the lives of those we care about, will be gone."
—*Don't Fear the Shark*, by Jonathan Kathrein

How did I find myself in the jaws of a shark? Don't things like this always happen to someone else?

It all began with my love of water. Growing up in Illinois, I dreamed of being a surfer. I had never seen the ocean, but I knew I loved it. I fell asleep at night listening to the Beach Boys and imagining I could hear the sound of crashing waves. When I was four years old, my friend Logan moved to San Diego. I thought of him surfing and wanted that to be me.

Looking back on the day of the attack, it was a formative day in my life. I think about the shark even now and I know I will never forget it. I'm married now and I have a child. As a husband and father, I appreciate life more fully through the unique perspective of my experience with the shark and my survival.

Wednesday, August 26, 1998
Stinson Beach, California

"LAST SHARK SIGHTING – Sunday, August 19." The sign at the edge of the beach attracted little attention. Most of the surfers rushed past without noticing it as they jogged to the water, boards tucked under their arms. The message fluttered on the salt-washed post. Shifting sands showed no footprints anywhere near it. Things had been quiet for the past few days. Stinson Beach with its white sand and gentle waves seemed an unlikely place to find the greatest predator of the deep.

Stinson Beach, north of San Francisco
on the California coast

Fog spread over the North Coast. Temperatures soared and summer heat scorched the inland valleys, but along the coast it stayed cool. Whitewater sprayed off the waves and strands of kelp had washed up onto the beach. The sky was grey. Waves offshore at Duxbury Reef could be seen from Stinson Beach. Wind swells were rolling into the beach with waves breaking close to shore. Powerful currents and tides swept along the coast. The Golden Gate Bridge was wrapped in fog. Cars jammed the roads to and from the beach.

The front page of the morning newspaper showed a surfer riding a wave with the headline, "Fog and Wind Advisory for the Coast." The photo showed an ocean that looked wild and windblown, but that was nothing new. Ocean currents here along the North Coast are almost always strong. It looked like a great day for surfing; I didn't want to miss it.

I was sixteen, enjoying the newfound freedom of my driver's license, and it was the last day of summer vacation. School would start the next day and I'd be a junior in high school. Now that I had my license, Mom let me start driving to the beach.

I checked the weather forecast and everything looked good. The National Weather Service had issued a fog advisory for the coast. It was a typical August day along the North Coast of California.

On the East Coast, Hurricane Bonnie made landfall with heavy rain and high surf lashing the coastline. High winds reached up to 115 mph and waves topped out as high as fifty-nine feet. Forecasters warned of severe weather everywhere in the East. Late summer weather could be volatile on every coast.

3

California surfers know the Pacific Ocean is mostly flat through the summer months, but Sean and I didn't mind. The more experienced surfers become hopeful and excitement increases when waves start to pick up in late August. At times, long-period swells might come off Japan or from a storm in New Zealand, bringing in some good surf. Conditions on the ocean could change in a few hours, or even minutes. We'd be happy to be at the beach no matter what. We were not experienced surfers, but we were eager to learn.

Early that morning I called the beach to ask the lifeguards about the latest conditions for Stinson Beach. From the tower they said the waves looked inconsistent, with an occasional solid peak and a moderate local wind. The recent swell was fading but it didn't really matter to me. My tide calendar, a paper booklet with the tide charts for each day, predicted it would be low tide when we got to the beach. Perfect for catching waves.

I always checked the conditions before heading out because the Pacific Ocean can be dramatic and unpredictable, with shifting weather, currents, and winds influencing the waves. On warm days, rising summer heat draws the fog in over the coast. In August, the Pacific can be flat or rough and it can change in a minute. Cold water and powerful waves can be treacherous for anyone who is not prepared. Unexpected things can happen and no one can predict what a day at the ocean will bring. Especially for a sixteen-year-old boy who had grown up in Illinois before moving to the coast.

I'd known Sean for two years, since our freshman year in high school. We met on the first day at St. Ignatius High

School in San Francisco and I liked him immediately. We'd been best friends ever since. I was glad Sean had decided to join me for the trip to the beach. We'd driven out to Stinson many times over the summer and it was our favorite place to spend a day. We always had fun together at the beach, spending hours in the water. We wanted to make the most of this day. Summer vacation was almost over; the next day we'd be back in school.

I cruised down the road that morning with my car loaded for a day at Stinson Beach. Breezing along the freeway with my windows down, my hair blowing in the wind, and my board in the back of my car, I was the happiest guy on the road, without a care in the world as I raced toward Mill Valley on my way to pick up Sean. The bright orange board in the back of my car would have been enough to catch any surfer's attention as I hurried along to the cutoff that would take me to Sean's house and then out to the beach.

Sean would be waiting for me, ready to go for a day of riding the waves. Generally, it was an hour to the coast over winding roads across the mountain and down the other side to the beach; but I was sure I could make it in less. I was in a hurry to get out to the beach.

I pulled into his driveway and gave a quick honk. Just as I expected, he rushed out the door, tossed an armload of gear in the back, and hopped into the car. In no time, we were on our way with our favorite Beach Boys music playing, eager to get to the beach. With all the traffic, I knew it was a day for the back roads heading west to the ocean.

Leaving Mill Valley we turned onto Montford Avenue at the old 2 am Club, a corner landmark. It was a popular hangout for locals, a gathering spot with pool tables, a neon sign, and dark windows. The door was always open and we passed it every time we went to Stinson, but we'd never taken time to step inside.

"C'mon Jon, hurry up, make this light."

"Don't worry, Sean, we'll save time by taking the shortcut. The beach will be there, waiting for us."

I watched the road from Mill Valley quickly narrow down to only two lanes. I followed the yellow center line, like a yellow brick road, around sharp curves that hugged the cliffs overlooking the Pacific. The shortcut was spectacular, winding around and over Mount Tamalpais, leading us through the trees and out to the beach. Sometimes we saw deer along the edge of the road, or families of California quail parading with their little feather topknots. Views of the ocean along the way were amazing; I could already see the waves.

The steep upward grade wound in and out of hairpin turns through the oak and redwood trees. Damp moss hung from the branches, almost touching the car, and the earth dropped away sharply at the edge of the road. At the top of the hill we entered into the drifting fog and escaped to another world. All thoughts of school vanished and we left our cares behind. To me, the beach was always beautiful, even in the fog.

Sean and I had explored the back roads together many times over the summer and discovered our favorite shortcut to the beach. Mom always worried because the curves were dangerous and even that morning she had reminded me to drive carefully. The funny thing was, she didn't worry so much about the ocean. She knew I was a strong swimmer with years of practice on the Lucas Valley and high school swimming and water polo teams. I'd passed the Red Cross lifesaving classes and worked as a lifeguard at our local neighborhood pool. I could handle the waves and I was not afraid of a little water in my face. Still, I was always cautious in the ocean and I didn't take unnecessary risks. Everyone knows that sharks live in the ocean, especially in the waters of what is called the "Red Triangle." But I'd never focused on the fact that the coastline of Northern California was also the coast of the Red Triangle.

The "Red Triangle" refers to a triangle-shaped geographic area of the Pacific Ocean along the coast of Northern California. It stretches approximately 100 miles from Monterey Bay in the south, to Bodega Bay in the north, and out to the Farallon Islands in the Pacific Ocean in the west. These waters are rich with marine life, especially seals, sea lions, and sea otters—favorite meals of the great white shark.

More great white sharks live here in the Red Triangle than anywhere else on Earth. And more shark attacks happen here than in any place in the world, more than in Australia or in South Africa. There are ten times more shark attacks in the Red Triangle than there are along the entire remainder of the California coastline. August through October are known as "shark season" in the Red Triangle, when most shark attacks happen. Late summer brings the sharks closer to shore as they follow the food supply brought to shore by the seasonal upwelling current.

The Red Triangle received its name because of the frequency of shark attacks, and the color of the water after

7

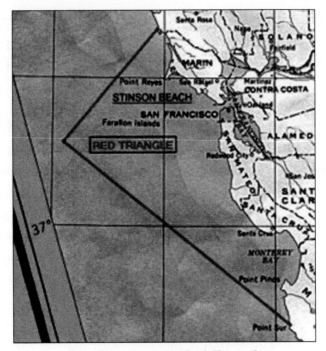

Area known as the Red Triangle

an attack. The abundance of white sharks first prompted divers to call it the "White Triangle." Later, with the number of attacks and the blood in the water, it became informally known as the "Red Triangle." Sometimes also called "Grand Central" for sharks, the area lives up to its name with an average of one to two shark attacks each year.

This infamous stretch of coastline encompasses many popular local beaches, including Stinson Beach, where we were headed. Known mostly to scientists, surfers, and locals, it's not widely known by name, and it's an area not generally designated on maps of the coast. The Red Triangle wasn't marked on any of my maps.

Good waves and beautiful beaches make the Red Triangle an irresistible place for surfing, in spite of its risks as a great white feeding zone. Good swells coming in from far out at sea create well-formed and rideable waves at the beaches along this coastline. The North Coast is known for its year-round good surfing and cold water.

Waves form near the shore when wind or storms out at sea create a disturbance on the surface of the ocean. The wind and air currents create movement in the water called "swells." The swells are huge masses of water that rise and fall with a gentle rolling motion. Swells do not break. They form waves that break when the water becomes too shallow, or when they hit a reef or the shallow ocean floor or a beach that interrupts the movement of the wave and causes it to crash.

I had never really heard about any shark sightings off the coast. An "unofficial" shark sighting was probably not even reported because it was a shark spotting that was undocumented and unconfirmed by lifeguards or park officials. Not every report was reliable because an untrained eye might mistake a dolphin, or even a seal, for a shark. To the trained eye, the triangular dorsal fin of the shark is distinguishable from the more pointed, curved fin of a dolphin. The size and shape of the fin could indicate whether it belonged to a dolphin or a great white shark. And sometimes a shark might just be cruising past and wouldn't stay around. No cause to close the beach.

Until the summer of my sixteenth year my life had been pretty predictable and nothing life-threatening had ever happened to me. Thinking about sharks out in the ocean didn't really worry me because I thought shark attacks were so rare that it was almost impossible it would ever happen to me. I knew sharks lived in the ocean, way out there somewhere. But I felt safe at the beach where I thought nothing could happen.

No one ever talked about seeing sharks at Stinson Beach. I had never heard of a shark attack there, or at any of the beaches I knew, and I would never have expected anyone to be attacked at the beach. In surfing, as with any sport, you take a few risks because you don't think bad things will ever really happen. I'd never envisioned my life being on the line, or having to fight for my next breath. But I knew as well as anyone that you've got to be smart in the ocean. The ocean is a living environment where conditions can change every minute.

I opened my eyes early that morning, too excited to sleep, thinking of our trip to the beach and about riding the waves. I watched the sun come through the fluttering leaves of the orange tree outside my bedroom window. My brother Eric was asleep in his bed next to mine and my brother Michael was sleeping in his room across the hall. The house was quiet but I was wide awake and eager to get going.

I jumped up, pulled on a t-shirt, and hurried down the hallway, headed for the kitchen. I moved quietly. For some reason this morning seemed different and exciting. I grabbed a bowl and the box of Grape-Nuts.

Before going to bed the night before, I had loaded my car with my wetsuit, boogie board, beach towel, water bottle, and wide-brimmed canvas hat. I enjoyed the preparation almost as much as the trip and wanted to be sure I remembered all the things I might need at the beach. I set my sunglasses and keys beside the kitchen door with my sandals, ready for the morning.

After breakfast, just as I was ready to go, my mother walked into the kitchen. I leaned over to give her a hug before I headed out the door.

"Bye, Mom. I'm heading out to pick up Sean. We'll be at Stinson all day."

"Okay. Bye, Jonathan." She brushed a kiss onto my cheek as I hurried past. "Have fun and drive carefully."

"I will. Bye, Mom," I called as the kitchen door slammed behind me. Then I noticed I'd forgotten my sandals so I stepped back inside, slid my feet into my flip-flops and turned once again toward the door.

"Bye again, Mom . . . love you."

"Bye, Jonathan. I love you, too."

This time the kitchen door slammed with finality, but Mom had already noticed my hesitation and she followed me out to my car. I don't know why, but leaving seemed to take forever that day. And for some reason we had a hard time saying goodbye.

"Jonathan, please be careful on the roads. And don't be late or I'll worry."

"I'll be careful. Don't worry, Mom." I knew she'd be expecting me for dinner and I didn't want her to worry. We'd planned a family gathering for dinner later that evening to celebrate the last day of summer.

Before climbing into the car I gave her one last hug. With so many goodbyes and the lingering farewell, I knew Mom was growing apprehensive about my going to the beach. She looked worried, standing beside my car in a white summer dress, lips pressed together as if holding back a tear. I'll never forget the look on her face. I could tell she didn't want me to go, but she didn't want to say

11

anything. I backed out of the driveway and turned onto the street.

"Bye, Mom." I shouted from my car window one last time, trying to ease her concern. "I'll see you later." My voice drifted down the street on the morning breeze. I'll never know why I said goodbye to my mom so many times. A curious feeling struck me as I drove off, but I didn't believe in premonitions so I didn't let it bother me.

I savored my freedom with the bittersweet joy that summer vacation was nearing an end and tomorrow I'd be in school. Heading for the beach that day reminded me of my childhood when summer days felt wonderfully long and aimless.

In my early days growing up in Illinois, we lived in a quiet neighborhood just two blocks from the little Tower Lakes Beach. The lake was small and calm with hardly a ripple. I took swimming lessons and learned to jump off the wooden dock into the water. Swimming out from shore gave me a sense of freedom.

I spent long summer days in the water with my brothers, Michael and Eric. Mom taught us that brothers are best friends and we were always together. We played sharks and minnows and Marco Polo with our friends laughing and splashing each other. The days were warm and I felt safe in the water even when I couldn't see what was beneath me. Oh, there were fish out there all right and they'd bite my legs, but I came to accept swimming with fish. I didn't bother them and, except for an occasional nibble, they didn't bother me. The lake was warm and safe, with no rip tides, rogue waves, or sharks to worry about.

Illinois, where I learned to swim

On warm summer evenings we played kick-the-can with all the neighborhood kids or caught lightning bugs and let them go. As the big brother, I'd watch out for Michael and Eric, and we used the buddy system to stick together. We explored the pond near our house, chased frogs, and played soccer on the field across the street. We were all-American kids growing up in a friendly neighborhood with lots of families, no streetlights, and hardly any traffic. We knew our neighbors and we never worried about locking our doors. It was a safe world that was friendly and predictable.

On weekends we took family trips to Madison to visit Grandma McClellan at her house on the edge of Lake Mendota, overlooking the Wisconsin state capitol. We spent warm summer days jumping off the pier, scattering the ducks, splashing and floating in the cool water near the shore. Little fish nibbled our toes and grass entangled our

*With Grandma on her pier, Lake Mendota,
Madison, Wisconsin*

Fishing on Grandma's pier, Lake Mendota, Madison, Wisconsin

legs in the water but I didn't mind. I loved the windblown days when the lake tossed and grew wild with bouncy whitecaps. And yet I dreamed of the ocean and surfing.

Much to my delight, my parents decided we'd move to California when my dad got a new job in San Francisco. We piled into the Olds Toronado with our cat, Mufti, and headed west. I remember how excited I was at the thought of seeing the ocean for the first time. Just the sound of it had a magical ring; I pictured warm, sunny beaches with surfers and palm trees. I couldn't wait to plunge into the ocean, ready for anything.

I loved the Pacific Ocean from the moment I saw it. For our first family outing at the beach we packed our sand buckets and swimsuits, expecting a warm sunny day at

*Water fun before the shark, visiting our grandparents
at Lake Hartwell, South Carolina*

the coast. As we drove over the winding roads and rolling hills, past farmland on the way to the coast, I waited with great anticipation for the ocean to appear. Finally when we arrived at Limantour Beach, on the coast of Point Reyes National Seashore, we were surprised to find waves pounding the shore, a cold wind blowing off the ocean, and fog drifting over the beach. It was not the sunny beach day we expected. Windblown waves crashed in the surf and rolled to shore. It was a mess, and I loved it.

Michael took the lead, running into the whitewater at the edge of the surf. Eric and I followed close behind him. When I felt the salty chill of the ocean and the power and excitement of the waves, my fascination grew. The Pacific Ocean was not what I had expected, but I was intrigued and curious.

Our weekend family trips to the beach continued, and I knew it was just the beginning. My brothers and I grew stronger and more adventurous as we grew older. We swam in the cold water until we felt numb, never minding the chill; the exhilaration of the ocean was captivating. Dad always watched cautiously when we were in the water, and Mom reminded us that brothers are best friends, always there for each other. Together, we were confident we could handle anything. We were strong and ready for new adventures.

With every trip to the coast, I grew to love the ocean more. The ocean became a part of my life and I became a part of the ocean. I relished the adventure as well as the solitude I found at the coast. I learned to appreciate the vastness of the ocean and I was intrigued by the mysteries of this wild and extreme world. I wanted the ocean to be a part of my life forever.

STINSON BEACH
Marin County California

"I must go down to the seas again, for the call of the running tide
Is a wild call and a clear call that may not be denied;
All I ask is a windy day with the white clouds flying,
And the flung spray and the blown spume, and the sea-gulls crying."
—"Sea Fever," by John Masefield

Sean and I were headed for Stinson Beach at the base
of Mount Tamalpais where coastal bluffs tower above the
coast and the wide sandy beach sweeps out to the great
Pacific. The beach stretches from a rocky point at the
south end to the mouth of Bolinas Lagoon at the north.
It's a picturesque three-mile-long crescent of sand that
hugs the edge of the North American continent only a
few miles north of the Golden Gate Bridge. Waves crash
against the shore, towering redwoods rise above the
coast, and windswept dunes lead out to the ocean. It's a
dramatic meeting of land and sea.

To get to Stinson Beach we first had to cross Mount
Tamalpais, the highest peak in Marin County. The

mountain was formed as the result of plate tectonic action, the collision of the North American and Pacific plates of the earth moving in opposite directions near the San Andreas Fault. The mountain is a familiar sight from all over Marin, with its recognizable peak rising 2,600 feet above sea level. According to the native Miwok legend, the silhouette of the mountain represents a sleeping maiden who waits for the god of the sun to return to earth.

The road was shady that morning and the route was familiar. I let the majesty of the road lead me forward. My head was filled with thoughts of cresting waves as I drove through a tunnel of fog into another world. Tall redwoods clustered in the narrow ravines along the road like shadowy giants, with only thin shafts of light penetrating their branches. California oaks and bay trees arched above us. I saw manzanita and chaparral bushes intertwined with poison oak clinging to the hillsides along the road. I lowered my window to feel the statuesque presence of the trees. The tangled fragrance of damp ferns and salty ocean air flooded through my open window and I knew we were nearing the ocean.

We approached the crest of Mount Tam where the road began to drop down toward the beach. As we rounded a wide curve at the top the wide Pacific Ocean suddenly sprawled across our view. From high above Stinson Beach I studied the surf, checking out the waves. I could see some nice waves rolling in and they were holding their shape well. The crescent-shaped beach was a strip of sand fringed with white foam along the shore. In the center of the beach I could see the familiar outline of the old blue lifeguard tower standing watch over the beach.

The sound of the thunderous surf floated up. Turkey vultures soared along the edge of the mountain, floating on invisible winds. From high above the beach I could see a vast world of water. I took a deep breath and watched the ocean rise and fall as one swell followed another. Each swell grew and folded upon itself, breaking into a thin line of whitewater. I watched the waves crashing against the beach. The blue-grey ocean faded into the distant sky obscuring the horizon in a hazy panorama of sky and water. On a clear day you could see the peaks of the Farallon Islands in the distance, but not today. A handful of surfers floated in the water near the shore, their black wetsuits shining like the wet fur of harbor seals.

We followed the wide curve of the road that swept down the mountain toward the coast. I slowed down as we approached the faded green sign marking the edge of

town, "Stinson Beach, Elevation 115." Beyond the sign, a thread of buildings lined the main street with small shops, restaurants, and galleries. Most of them were still closed but they'd be open later and the town would be bustling. A handful of people gathered outside on the wooden deck near the café in the middle of the block, their coffee steaming into the morning air.

Although isolated by its location, Stinson has become a popular coastal beach town over the years and is now visited by millions of people annually. The drama of the ocean landscape and the unpredictability of its weather increase the spirit of isolation and adventure along the coast.

"Sean, let's stop at Live Water Surf Shop and you can rent a wetsuit."

"I might not need it today. Anyway, I don't really want to pay for it."

"Let's get the wetsuit so you can stay out longer. The water is always cold."

Though not far from San Francisco, the town of Stinson felt like a different world. It gave us a sense of adventure. Even during the busy summer months it managed to keep its quaint, small-town feel with only a few shops and restaurants, but not a single gas station. It was an outpost for recreation with parkland, forest, and ocean on all sides and little chance for major growth. The mood of the town could be as unpredictable as the ocean, lively or peaceful, even in August. The town seemed especially quiet that day as we entered the world of the coast.

I shifted into low gear as we drove along a street lined with weathered storefronts, picket fences, painted rocks, and wooden carvings. Shells and treasures from the beach decorated the yards and windows. Weather vanes turned their faces into the wind. A row of colorful surfboards and boogie boards leaned against the side of the building outside the café. I was happy to be at the coast as the day began to unfold.

I'd heard that Stinson was originally an early tourist destination called "Willow Camp," with tents under the willow trees along the beach. The Mill Valley and Mount Tamalpais Railroad brought visitors from San Francisco to the beach by ferry, train, and stagecoach. Stinson Beach became its official name in 1916. With the completion of the Golden Gate Bridge in 1937, Stinson Beach became an even more popular destination for San Franciscans trying to escape the summer fog and for locals who love the ocean.

I was happy to have one last summer day at the beach. I wished Michael and Eric could have joined me for this trip. They loved the water as much as I did, but Michael was busy with freshman orientation on his first day of high school at St. Ignatius, and Eric was getting ready to start school at Miller Creek Middle School. Maybe on the weekend we could plan a family trip.

The Live Water Surf Shop in the center of town was open early, making it an easy stop for surfers to pick up wetsuits, boards, and beach gear. The owners always knew the latest surf conditions as well as the local news. The shop's "No Shark" stickers with a red slash through the words had become a popular symbol and souvenir of Stinson Beach. I pulled up at the curb in front of the shop.

"I'll wait while you run in to get a wetsuit," I said.

"Okay, I'll be right out," Sean slammed the car door and sprinted toward the shop.

"Get some shark stickers too," I called after him.

In a few minutes Sean returned empty-handed, looking disappointed. "They said I couldn't rent a wetsuit because I'm not eighteen."

"I'm surprised. Why do they care?"

"Maybe they're afraid they'd be responsible if I got attacked by a shark. Anyway, never mind, Jonathan, I just won't wear one today. It's not a big deal. And I'm only kidding about the shark."

"Okay. I guess you'll be fine in the water without it for a while, but you'll get cold out there."

"Well, let's give it a try."

We continued through town past the Parkside Café. It was a popular snack bar, with a window at the edge of the sand where they served the best burgers and malts in town. It was our favorite hangout at the beach and often the line stretched around the corner on a busy summer afternoon. I wasn't sure why, but the usually busy corner looked empty this time as we passed.

Sean and I were hoping for some good waves to ride and some excitement in the water. Reef and beach breaks create dynamic waves along the North Coast of California. Waves follow the contour of the ocean, breaking when the water becomes shallow. The Pacific near San Francisco is colder and the waves are rougher than those in southern California, but surfers love the invigorating challenge of North Coast surfing.

On a good day, we could see waves breaking out at Duxbury Reef, an area of the Pacific located a mile offshore from Stinson, near the southern tip of Point Reyes National Seashore. It's one of the largest shale reefs in North America and part of a network of protected areas dedicated to preserving a diverse ocean habitat consisting of rocky and soft bottom, shallow rocky reefs, and kelp beds. A wild area where whitewater crashes, it's home to marine mammals, seabirds, invertebrates, algae, and fish, including white sharks, not far from the beach.

Memories of family picnics and beach days over the years came to mind as I drove through Stinson. The chill of the air didn't surprise me. Summer days at the coast could be cool, while a few miles inland, beyond the fog, the day might be hot and sunny. Rising heat in inland valleys leaves a vacuum in its wake that pulls the fog over the coast. It was one of those days. Summer was fading and the crowds had gone. Families were probably busy getting ready for school. The beach was quiet and memories lingered in summer scrapbooks.

Experts say sharks are not looking to interfere with humans in the water. Our shark attack fears are irrational. We all know we're more likely to be struck by lightning than attacked by a shark. But for most people, fiery emotions override even the coldest facts. Shark attacks strike a sort of fear in our souls and elicit a universal awe. A single scary shark story can capture headlines for weeks and override the efforts of scientists trying to communicate research and logic.

Violence and wild animals, together with the magnificent backdrop of the ocean, resonate with intense drama

that strikes our souls. Sharks never fail to inspire terror and, even at the same time, to fascinate us. The para-
dox between our fear and our logic may explain our love
of sharks. E. O.Wilson, a Harvard professor and biologist
known for theories of social behavior, has observed:

> We're not just afraid of predators, we're transfixed
> by them, prone to weave stories and fables and
> chatter endlessly about them, because fascination
> creates preparedness, and preparedness, survival.
> In a deeply tribal sense, we love our monsters.

Just up the coast to the north, Stinson Beach meets
the opening where the ocean enters into the wide Bolinas
Lagoon.

Bolinas Lagoon is an internationally significant wetland
with over 1,000 acres of tidal estuary rich in nutrients and
marine life. The lagoon encompasses an important coastal
environment with rich biodiversity that provides a habitat
for fish, water birds, and marine mammals. It's a safe haul-
out for seals, with warmer water and a shoreline protected
by the surrounding wetlands. Shore birds, ducks, herons,
and egrets nest around the lagoon while seals and sea lions
sun themselves along its shores. A thin spit of land protects the shallow lagoon from the Pacific Ocean. The mouth
of the lagoon flows to the sea with the tide moving quickly,
allowing the lagoon to take in seawater on rising tides and
exchange it for a mixture of fresh and seawater on low tide.
An average of three million cubic yards of water flows
between the ocean and the lagoon with each tide.

Great White Shark

The lagoon is like a spa for seals, with sharks waiting in the parking lot. Great white sharks swim just outside the mouth of the lagoon waiting for seals, salmon, and other prey to move out into the ocean from upstream.

Bolinas Beach is a nearby popular surf spot with waves breaking along the coast that are known to be moderate enough even for beginners. Several surf camps offer lessons here. Some of my friends liked to surf at Bolinas, but I never wanted to try it because I'd heard rumors of sharks. Some surfers referred to the mouth of the lagoon as "shark alley" and a Google search for information on Bolinas would reveal a photo of a great white shark. From the coastline at Bolinas, the Farallon Islands are only twenty miles offshore. Even with its reputation for sharks, Bolinas Beach was a popular local surfing choice.

Although the town of Bolinas is only two miles up the coast, just beyond the north end of Stinson Beach, driving from Stinson to Bolinas is six miles, with the road winding around the broad lagoon. Bolinas has always been known for the seclusion of its residents and the difficulty others have in finding the town. With few signs marking the turnoff, it feels like a remote beach town and the little-known road is traveled mainly by locals and surfers headed for the beach. The road scarcely offers room to turn around at the end.

We took our time cruising through the town of Stinson, checking out the scene. In the center of town I turned at a big green sign that read, "Stinson Beach Parking." We followed the wide driveway into a big parking lot that looked mostly deserted. There were hardly any cars and the pavement was dusted with blowing sand. I parked near the sandy path and we jumped out.

"I'm glad we're here early. We'll have plenty of time to catch some waves," I said.

"Pop the trunk and let's get our gear," Sean replied. He slid the two boards out and leaned them against the side of the car. I grabbed my blue canvas duffle bag, my hooded sweatshirt, and my water bottle. Our boards looked colorful standing there together. Sean's was bright blue and mine was darker blue with an orange bottom.

"Hey, don't forget your towel," I reminded him.

He pulled out his thick blue and yellow towel, the one he always brought on our trips to the beach, and tossed it over his shoulder. The big towel would feel good after being out there in the cold water.

I slipped my keys into my pocket and slammed the trunk. The sound of the trunk slamming marked the closing of one world and the opening of another. We left the outside world and its cares behind and headed for the ocean.

The sound of our flip-flops broke the morning stillness as our footsteps echoed across the sand-covered blacktop. At the edge of the parking lot we followed the path leading up and over the dunes to the beach. Loose sand slipped away underfoot with each step. I took off my sandals to feel the sand on my bare feet. The cool, moist sand with its rough texture felt good against my feet with each stride. Even with all the gear we carried, the trek seemed easy as we hurried up the dunes, eager to check out the waves.

The sand cooled my feet and the air felt fresh, but there was no warmth in the breeze. A scrub jay shrieked from the bushes to warn of our approach. The fog chilled our faces and beach grass brushed our legs. The day seemed refreshing and inviting.

At the top of the dunes the Pacific Ocean broke into view before us. We stood there, mesmerized for a moment, without a word, gazing out at the beach. I took a deep breath, savoring the musty fragrance of saltwater mingled with kelp, my senses aware of every detail. The sights and sounds of the ocean were comforting and familiar. The ocean filled our view and seemed to stretch forever. I was happy to be at the coast.

The faded blue lifeguard tower stood watch over the beach just as it did every day, quiet and undisturbed in the early light. It was a well-known landmark and always the meeting place for friends at Stinson Beach. With its balcony and sparkling windows encircling the top like a crown, the tower cast its familiar silhouette on the beach. Coastal bluffs loomed like distant citadels. Beach grass rustled in the shadows of the dunes beneath the tower.

I made a visual sweep to check out the conditions of the water, the sky, and the weather coming in. I was as cautious at the ocean as I was at the little Tower Lakes beach where I first learned to swim. I watched the spray blowing off the tops of the waves and the ripples of foam flowing across the sand and back out to sea. Life always seemed to have a different rhythm at the coast. I slowed down to enjoy the day.

The waves looked good, with swells rolling in from the horizon. I was happy to see the good surf because I knew Point Reyes, a point of land to the north, blocked the north swell at Stinson, sometimes weakening the waves at the beach to almost nothing.

Stinson Beach lifeguard tower

On the horizon, I saw the faint outline of a cargo ship cutting through the fog and heading for San Francisco. Pelicans followed each other in a wobbly line, skimming low across the water and looking for food. Seagulls flew up on the beach in a sudden display of excitement, probably fighting over someone's lunch left unattended on the beach. It was a fine day, although visibility was poor and the water looked unsettled. But that was okay. Long strands of kelp and sea grass were strewn across the sand, brought to shore by the current and the swells. Two fishing boats rocked from side to side in the choppy water near the beach. Seeing the boats so close to shore seemed unusual but I didn't give them much thought. Seagulls swarmed above the boats, screaming and eager for scraps. The tide was low and the waves were breaking on the rocks at the far end of the beach. I saw the black head of a seal pop up in the surf and then disappear just as quickly into the water.

RACE TO THE OCEAN

"It's opener there in the wide open air.
Out there things can happen and frequently do. . . ."
—*Oh, the Places You'll Go!* by Dr. Seuss

We ran down the dunes like restless racehorses, our bare feet digging into the sand. Bouncing down the face of the dunes with long legs and long strides, we were moon-walkers free of gravity. Sand flew up in all directions. We found a good spot where the beach leveled out, tossed our towels on the sand, and leaned our boards against an old redwood log. The old log had no doubt witnessed similar scenes from long ago along the coast. Two surfers in black wetsuits jogged past us carrying their boards and rushing to the water. Sean stared out at the waves and seemed distracted.

"I thought I saw something," he said, "but I guess it was only a shadow in the water or a seal."

A swell rose and then crashed into a thundering wave. Two soccer players passed a ball at the water's edge. I heard a foghorn calling from somewhere near the Golden Gate. It was a typical morning at Stinson Beach.

I reached into my bag and pulled out my wetsuit. It was a spring suit with short sleeves and short legs, not as thick as the full wetsuits most surfers wore, but it would help to keep out the chill. I stepped into the wetsuit and pulled the unforgiving neoprene up over my shoulders.

I remembered how my brothers and I had found the wetsuit at a neighborhood garage sale. We ran home to count our money and ask Mom if it would be okay. The price was right, and Mom agreed, thinking of the fun we'd have at the beach. The wetsuit had lasted for years, longer than I'd expected, but it was getting too small for me and I'd need a new one soon. I grabbed the cord and zipped it up my back to my neck. Sean was wearing only his blue swimsuit and a faded grey t-shirt. We both knew he'd get cold, but we were so excited we couldn't wait to plunge into the chilly water. I was glad to have my shorty wetsuit.

One of the biggest obstacles to surfing in Northern California is the harshness of the elements, especially the cold water. Water temperatures range from forty-three to fifty-five degrees Fahrenheit year round. Northern California surfers need a wetsuit to stay in the water and keep warm in the cold ocean conditions. A good wetsuit can make a big difference in fifty-five-degree water. My wetsuit was thin, but it would help.

Newer high-performance stretch neoprene is a light-weight material that provides warmth, flexibility, and free-dom to paddle and ride the waves. For winter surfing, some surfers wear hoods, boots, and gloves; others prefer to feel the cold salty water and wind on their feet and heads.

For the brutally cold water of Northern California, most surfers wear full body 4/3 neoprene wetsuits. These wetsuits have a chest thickness of four millimeters with an arm and leg thickness of three millimeters. The thousands of tiny air bubbles embedded in the neoprene material work to prevent heat loss and provide thermal insulation. In addition, the wetsuit fills with water that creates a thin layer of insulation between the skin and the suit. Just as a person's body warms the air inside a sweatshirt, the surfer's body warms the layer of water inside the wetsuit, creating an effective barrier against the cold.

My wetsuit wasn't very thick, and it didn't fully cover my legs and arms. I'd still feel the cold, but the wetsuit would allow me to stay in the water a little longer. Sean didn't seem to mind going without a wetsuit, but he wouldn't be able to stay in the water as long as I would before getting cold.

The beach was wide and spacious, and the air was soft. At sixteen, we had no worries, no school, and no schedule. We could stay in the water all day.

We watched the next wave, trying to judge where the waves were breaking. A surfer hit the lip, shot across the crest, and crashed into the foam. He popped up quickly for another ride.

"This looks great," Sean said.

"Okay, let's go."

Together we took off running and sprinted to the edge of the water, scattering shore birds in every direction. A crowd of gulls floated over our heads and then landed further down the beach. We ignored their raucous cries, or perhaps failed to understand their warning.

Running to the water with the coarse sand against my feet brought back memories of my childhood and friends at the safety of the little beach where I grew up in Illinois. Memories of a perfect beach day could last a lifetime. This was the ocean I'd dreamed of then.

Standing at the edge of the water, the ocean looked even higher than the land. I looked up to the thin line where the ocean met the sky. Swells rose and the ocean beckoned us forward, reminding us it was always there.

We hit the cold water and splashed in ankle-deep. I tossed my board across the water and flopped onto it. The ocean flooded into my wetsuit and the rush of cold water took my breath away. It was a feeling I loved. I forgot everything else and I was one with the ocean.

We plunged forward into the surf, letting the cold water toss us like strands of kelp. Surfing in the Pacific could be exhausting, yet invigorating, and the waves were always more powerful than they looked. We felt confident but yet so insignificant against the power of the ocean.

We paddled ahead with enthusiasm, diving headfirst into each wave, heading out away from shore into a world unchanged by time. It was a journey from civilization into freedom, a different journey for everyone. I dove down to feel the water in my hair and the chill refreshed me.

We moved steadily away from shore, pulling and kicking through each oncoming wave. We were confident in our abilities and the security of the beach we knew so well. As we moved further from shore, I noticed the water growing darker, but its obscurity didn't disturb me. Dark water was typical of the Pacific along the North Coast.

"Hey, Jonathan. Let's get out past this break," Sean shouted over the thundering whitewater.

"Okay, keep going, I'm with you."

We pushed ahead into each new wave, laughing, paddling, and struggling against the cold water. I launched myself forward. Saltwater hit my face and foam poured over my head. I felt the freedom and exhilaration of the ocean.

Sean dove forward into a wave. I watched and waited for him to reappear. When he didn't surface right away, I searched the water, wondering what had happened. I didn't want to admit I was worried. Suddenly a seal popped up and I saw Sean swimming beyond it, in the deeper water.

"Hey, Sean. Always stay inside the seals. You never know, something might be chasing them." We laughed and paddled and kept going.

Together we paddled hard to get through the waves until finally we were well beyond the break where a few surfers were relaxing on the swells, enjoying the ocean. The line of surfers was well spread out over a wide area. It was not a crowded day and looking back to shore, the beach looked nearly deserted. We relaxed and floated and watched the incoming waves.

In six feet of water fifty yards from shore the surface of the ocean was calm. I couldn't see the bottom but that was okay. The shadowy water was typical of the Pacific along the North Coast so it didn't bother me.

I thought about how powerless we were against the strength of the ocean and I realized how vulnerable and unprotected I was out there, but I was cautious and I knew I could swim to shore. Cold water splashed my face and my toes were numb. Nothing unusual for Northern California surfers.

Bigger sets were starting to roll in and I waited for a good one. The water was flat and still between the sets, and the waves seemed far apart with long flat spells. I wondered why it was such a small crowd in the water today. Maybe people had stayed home to get ready for school or maybe they were waiting for the sun to come out later in the day. I was glad Sean was with me, but we'd drifted apart.

The ocean appeared calm, quiet, and peaceful, but the stillness of the water could be deceiving. Northern California surfers sometimes notice a feeling they call *sharkiness*. It's that sense that causes the hair to rise on the back of the neck, the feeling you get when you're the last one out in the lineup, waiting for a final wave after the sun has set and something disturbs the surface. It's the feeling surfers get when they swear they see something, a large shadow in the gloom, but at second look nothing is there.

From the water, I watched the fog lighten. The sky began to clear ever so slightly as I floated and waited for a wave, hoping for a good one. I checked my watch, a birthday gift from my parents. It was still early. Plenty of time to enjoy the day.

Looking back to shore from the water, I could see the lifeguard tower standing tall above the sand. Solitary and shrouded in fog, the tower dominated the beach with its reassuring presence. The door was open and one of the guards stood on the deck with binoculars looking out at the ocean, calmly scanning the water. I could see Pat, the head lifeguard, climbing the stairs to the tower in his red shorts and flip-flops. His t-shirt looked faded from many days in the sun. The word "Guard" was visible in bold letters across his chest.

Bobbing up and down on the surface with my favorite board, I rocked back and forth in the salty ocean swells, waiting to catch the next wave. Only a few surfers were out there with us. A foghorn sounded from somewhere in the distance.

The ocean pulled me into a world of freedom. Being out in the waves and far from shore helped put things into perspective and gave me a chance to think. Then I noticed I was drifting, and I paddled gently against the current to stay in the center of the beach, directly out from the tower.

The California Current is one of the world's major ocean surface currents. It moves from north to south along the northern coastline of California, and then flows into the North Equatorial Current. About ten percent of the water in the ocean moves in surface currents. Water flows horizontally in the uppermost 400 meters of the ocean's surface, driven mainly by wind friction. Most surface currents move water above the pycnocline, the zone where the density of the water changes rapidly with depth. Deep ocean currents bring cold water to the shore.

The continental shelf, the submerged outer edge of the coast, slopes to the deep-sea floor, the ocean basin. Most of the material comprising the shelf comes from erosion of the adjacent continental mass. The continental slope is the transition to the true edge of the continent. In the Pacific, the continental margins at the edges of converging plates are called active margins because of their earthquake and volcanic activity. The Pacific Ring of Fire, a zone of seismic and volcanic activity, encircles the Pacific Ocean.

Extreme conditions and weather changes that summer had impacted the ocean. Global weather cycles known as El Niño and La Niña brought unusual water temperatures and changing conditions worldwide. Scientists recorded warm surface water that changed course. Colder deep-sea water flowed to the surface where nutrients in the water became more plentiful, and evaporation decreased, reducing cloud formation and rain. Water temperatures rose and some fish usually found further south appeared in the waters off the coast of Northern California. The convergence of these environmental conditions and events could undoubtedly influence the currents in the ocean as well as the behavior of the fish.

Surfers in dark wetsuits bobbed in the water not far from me, enjoying the wait. I watched the line of dark shapes on their boards, floating as one with the ocean. Hills rising above the coast looked like reflections of the ocean. A hang glider floated on the updraft near the cliffs.

The next big wave came and all the surfers scrambled into position, trying to judge where it would break, ready to match the speed of the wave, hoping the energy of the wave would catch their boards and push them forward. Suddenly a huge black fin cut through the water without warning, not more than fifteen feet from the line of surfers.

"Shark!" I heard a voice shout.

"Heads up! Quick, start paddling."

In a split second, everyone was scrambling, paddling hard, digging into the water with strong arms. Boards moved forward, gaining speed. One of the surfers lost control, his board flew up and he wiped out. Arms and feet splashed and flailed everywhere in the dark choppy water. Not much hope to get away out in the ocean, so far from safety. No way for anyone to escape something moving so fast and so close.

Within seconds the enormous black body arched up out of the water. Suddenly, another creature appeared beside the first. My breath returned in halting gasps. Two huge dolphins breached the line of surfers, so close you could look them in the eye. At last we could all take a breath and admire the dolphins with a huge sigh of relief. No reason to be alarmed after all. Worries faded into the excitement of the day. All the boards turned again and the surfers paddled out into the waves. False alarm. Anyway, the surf was picking up.

THE ART OF SURFING

"It's a big wilderness,
and there are wild animals out there."
—Golden Gate National
Recreation Spokesman

Surfing is a sport that lets you ride pure energy. A wave of energy moving through the water pushes your board across the surface. Riding this wave of energy is an unforgettable moment. For these time-warped seconds, life is pure. Surfing can change your life forever. For most surfers it becomes a passion with lifelong challenges.

Ocean swells move across the seas in deep water. As the swells arrive near their shallow-water destination such as a beach, reef, or sandbar, they begin shoaling, or stacking up on one another. They take on the fascinating look of corduroy—they slow down, their height increases, and the distance between them decreases, until they form breaking waves . . . energy released.

Waves rise and break in rhythmic patterns. The size and speed of each wave depends on the size of the swell, its speed, the interval between swells, how the winds are blowing, water depth, and the contour of the ocean bottom. Mavericks, for example, north of Half Moon Bay in Northern California, is known for epic winter waves that routinely crest at over twenty-five feet, and can top out at over eighty feet. With its bottom contour and depth, waves will not even begin to break until the swells reach ten to fourteen feet, moving at fifteen or more second intervals.

Surfers float in the surf watching the swells roll by, waiting for whatever Mother Nature has to offer, until they see a good one. A surfer will "drop in" as the wave begins to break. The wave grabs the board and rushing water propels it down the face of the wave with speed and energy. Surfers carve and skim across the rushing water until all the energy dissipates and the wave collapses into foam. Surfers dream of catching a barrel and riding inside the curl of the wave, encapsulated by its sheer energy. Riding the barrel is the coveted accomplishment of surfing.

Waves in the ocean keep coming, never stopping, with different sizes, shapes, and speeds. Every ride is different with new challenges. Whether you fly across the crest in a spectacular spray or glide quietly on the whitewater, the ride is the thrill.

Scientists have shown the positive effects of the ocean on human physiology. Something happens in the presence of the ocean—breathing and heart rate slow. The ocean calms and renews our senses. In surfing, riding a wave requires pinpointed concentration similar to the intense focus of deep meditation. Some neuroscientists theorize that with surfing, as with meditation, certain areas of the brain become calm and a spiritual consciousness may be achieved with the combination of the adrenaline rush of catching a wave and the intense concentration required to ride the wave.

Surfing, like life, is full of highs and lows, excitement and terror, fun and frustration. Learning to control or adapt to these variables can help you prepare for them. The challenge begins with your mind. Peace, power, calm, and focus are critical. To achieve these qualities, you must train and get your mind to a state of awareness.

Surfing is an extreme sport quite simply because you're on a moving field, one that changes every moment. The ocean and the conditions are never the same. This is where personality, preference, and patience kick in. Some surfers are content to relax; others seek a challenge.

Surfing presents a unique set of challenges. Catching a wave requires focus on the present moment. As with any extreme sport, intense concentration diminishes other distractions. The ocean is infinite and unpredictable, engaging your mind and body in unexpected ways.

You step into the water and jump onto your board, aware of the wind in your face, sun in your eyes, and a spray of fine droplets of water against your skin. The rest becomes a blur—an overwhelming of senses. At first that's the fun . . . being overpowered, and probably pretty safe.

From here you gain awareness. That's where the real satisfaction begins and where the challenge lies, the real allure of surfing. You begin to add levels or layers of consciousness. This part of the journey doesn't ever end. To become better at surfing, and to have more fun at the sport year after year, you must gain awareness of the world around you.

Like meditation, and life in general, you seek a deeper understanding. Much of this comes from cutting through the noise to become conscious of the present, and ready for the very immediate future.

Many people don't realize until they try that surfing is mostly paddling. You feel each hand enter the cold water as you paddle, dunk, dunk, dunk . . . your fingers chill with each stroke. Splash, and you can't see through the whitewater from a wave that passes over your head. And the waves just keep coming. No time to rest. In the ocean you can never let your guard down; a new wave is approaching.

If you dare to open your eyes, you see greenish-blue foam and sand swirling around you. Suddenly you're inside a Christmas snow globe an excited child has shaken too hard. If the waves are large enough, it's not uncommon to spend forty-five minutes paddling to get out through the breaking waves to calm water where you can finally rest. Some days are spent here.

Paddling requires strength and determination to move ahead against the force of oncoming waves, strong winds, and harsh currents. You lie motionless on the board, head up and toes pointed, trying to glide fast and straight across the top of the water without tipping the board. Speed, with little resistance from the sleek board, propels the board over the incoming swells. When waves are too large for a surfer to float over the top, he pushes the nose of the board down and through each wave. Joy, fear, and exhaustion clear your mind as you struggle to stay in control.

The awareness is something like this: crash, the wave explodes onto itself as it breaks; the spinning water rolls over you and you can't see. You're underwater now. Sometimes the water is so cold you get an ice cream headache. Your lungs begin to crave air. Then they start to tighten, and you fight a gulp, because you'd only get water anyway. Your body says, "Breathe," your mind says, "Please don't." You think you can't go any longer without air. Your board's being yanked from your hands as you spiral underwater. A cold current of water flushes your wetsuit. Finally, you surface.

Immediately, you see the next wave coming at you as you grab your board from the length of its fully extended leash. You scramble onto the board, arms aching from the paddle, and start the countdown again . . . 7 . . . 6 . . . paddle, paddle . . . 5 . . . 4 . . . keep going. Take a deep breath. Experience teaches you, as you gain awareness of your body and your environment, that despite the looming discomfort or just plain fear of the next wave, this is no time to hyperventilate. Breathe deep, and clear your lungs. Relax your heart rate so you burn oxygen more slowly. Calm your body . . . 3 . . . 2 . . . paddle, paddle, breathe. Your arm muscles are burning, especially your triceps. Your lower back is tight and tired.

The wave stands up tall as you fight your body to remain calm. You fill your lungs . . . and then . . . the wave annihilates itself right in front of you. This time you have the timing and presence of mind to push your arms down on the front of the board, sinking it, and then push a foot down on the back. You dive under the wave like a duck and propel yourself forward. The wave passes overhead. You pop up behind the wave and the water is calm. You can see the smooth surface of the water and bubbles coming up from the passing wave. You look to your right to see other surfers emerge, like beings stepping into another dimension. They look calm and untouched. You push ahead and continue to paddle hard. You're out here to catch a wave.

Oncoming waves rise up gently and then crash at just the perfect speed, peeling along the coast. To catch a wave, you dig your arms into the rushing water to match the speed of the wave and hang weightless at the crest for just a second before sliding down the face into the freedom of the wave. Nothing compares to being lifted on the rising swell, catching the speed of the wave, and racing down the face as it breaks. The ride is pure exhilaration.

Waves are amazing and breathtaking, especially when they surround you. The speed of each wave depends on its wavelength, with the longest waves moving fastest. The Pacific has the largest fetch, or distance, creating space between waves and the best chance for perfect waves to form. The waves are dynamic, always changing, following the contour of the ocean. This, along with the speed and size of the moving water, gives the wave its shape and form. A surfer on a wave traces the changing wave pattern, turning, bending, breaking, and pushing forward.

Before heading out, surfers check websites like Surfline.com, wannasurf.com, or the NOAA buoy report, to know what conditions to expect. The direction and size of the swell determines where the waves will break and the shape of the waves when they break.

Wind also affects waves. A northwest wind is the prevailing wind along the North Coast; a south wind can make the waves bumpy and difficult to ride. If the wind dies off at sunset, calm air produces a "glass off" perfect for surfing.

Surfers prefer an "offshore wind" that blows off the land into the oncoming surf, creating smooth water, helping the waves hold their shape. This "offshore wind" holds waves up and gives cleaner, more consistent waves. An "onshore wind" blows toward the shore, hitting the crest of the wave and creating messy, choppy water. A "side wind" can be favorable because it can produce conditions similar to the offshore wind. Some surfers will brave any conditions, even when the surf is choppy and the waves are blown out, because they love the ocean and the challenge.

Surfing can lead to spirituality in unique ways, by developing respect for nature and a sense of adventure. The freedom and simplicity of surfing, love of nature, harmony of the universe, fragility of our environment, and oneness of all things are unmistakable in the ocean. "Morning Mass" my brother Michael calls our morning surf sessions.

Surfing can increase confidence and personal development, offering satisfaction and time to think clearly in the open air. The ocean brings freedom and simple pleasures—water, fresh air, and sky, while being one with the ocean. The ocean fills your world with its force and power and eliminates other distractions. Being in the water is an escape from the stress of the world and a chance to think about what's important in life.

Surfing is great conditioning, requiring strength and agility to paddle out through powerful incoming waves, and fortitude to swim back out after every ride. Surfing takes practice, concentration, and timing. It unites mind, body, and spirit because it requires physical exertion and concentration.

The beaches of California's North Coast are known for big waves with good surf most of the year. Although waves and the ocean are symbols of stability in our lives, waves are not static. The rhythm and energy of the ocean can change in a moment, like the thundering rush of an avalanche, challenging even the best surfers. Waves and conditions in the ocean are always changing. Conditions along the North Coast are dramatic, wind and waves come from all directions, the surf is cold and dangerous, but surfers are rewarded with challenging surfing, beautiful scenery, and frequent sightings of dolphins, whales, and harbor seals.

Stinson Beach in Marin County is fifteen miles north of the Golden Gate Bridge along California's Highway 1, the famous scenic route along the coast. Stinson is considered a safe family beach with barbeque grills, showers, and waves breaking less than head high except in stormy weather. It's the northernmost beach in California with lifeguards on duty. The beach is a popular destination for picnics and swimming on a summer day, but cold water often promotes fog. Stinson Beach had no recorded shark attacks prior to 1998, despite its proximity to the Farallon Islands and its location at the edge of the Red Triangle.

A BLUR OF SPEED
AND POWER

"In an instant Jonathan's joy turned to panic. . . .
The next seconds would decide if he lived or died."
—*KNBC Channel 4 News*, LA

The noon whistle sounded its steady pitch over the roar of the waves. From the water I could hear it wailing in the distance, a reminder that this was the last day of summer and school would start tomorrow. The familiar call of the whistle didn't signal any reason to hurry the day; it simply marked the time, just as it did every day exactly at noon.

I watched the horizon rise and fall above the incoming swells. I was ready to go on the next good wave. For the moment, I was captivated by the sounds of the ocean and lost in the rhythm of the rolling swells.

Sean's voice brought me out of my reverie. "Hey Jonathan, I'm heading in to the beach to warm up."

"Okay, I'll catch one more wave and ride it in to join you."

Without another word Sean turned toward the beach and I turned back to face the sea. After Sean swam away,

I hardly noticed how alone I was. The other surfers had drifted away or caught a wave. Before me spread the great ocean. I felt safe fifty yards from shore, directly off the beach and within easy view of the tower.

Waves were rolling in and I paddled to catch the next one but it slipped by and I floated over the top. I was not thinking about the cold water. Or the Red Triangle. Or how easy it was for a shark to mistake a surfer for a seal.

The water was cool and the air was soft. My legs dangled beneath my board, fluttering in the water, suspended over the wide ocean floor. I was detached from the rest of the world, floating, waiting for the next ride, and watching the waves. I let the surf pull me out and I watched the day unfold. The vacant surface of the ocean didn't worry me.

All at once I felt the chill of the water and noticed how alone I was out there with no one anywhere around me. The ocean current was moving me steadily along the coast and I had drifted past the lifeguard tower. To keep from drifting too far, I began to paddle and kick against the current to get back to the center of the beach.

Suddenly, when I reached down to take my next stroke my hand bumped something underwater. I didn't know what it was. It felt solid and rough, like a big pile of sand. But the water was too deep to touch a pile of sand, and I knew there were no sandbars.

I looked around, wondering what it was, trying to think of every possibility. The water looked empty and mysterious. I didn't want to admit I was spooked. My thoughts raced as I searched for an answer. Maybe it was a jellyfish, but jellyfish are soft and they move when you touch them. This was firm and unyielding. Maybe it was a seal. I hoped to see a seal pop up near me, but nothing appeared. There were no seals, and even the pair of dolphins we'd seen earlier had disappeared. My hopes quickly dissolved. I was surrounded by vacant water. Nothing broke the surface of the water, and yet I knew something was out there with me.

The water spread before me into dark emptiness. The surface showed no sign of danger. A wide expanse separated me from the shore. I was completely alone and far from shore, easy prey for any predator in the ocean. This was a nightmare I had never expected. I wished Sean hadn't gone back to the beach.

My fear intensified and I felt every muscle tighten. The cold descended around me and penetrated every muscle. I was terrified. Something was terribly wrong. Suddenly the ocean was terrifying and unforgiving. I'd never been so afraid. My heart pounded and I feared the worst. Nothing could compare to the terror of being alone in the open water.

I knew I was swimming with a shark and it was coming back for me. While I was waiting for a wave, I'd become the target. I dreaded what was about to come.

I dared not panic; I had to hold it together if I wanted to have any hope of getting out alive. The water around me filled with shadows. Fear gripped my stomach. Terror changed my world. I shivered and turned inward to concentrate my strength. The smell of the saltwater, the summer sky, and the shimmering fog all became a blur. The beach looked far away. I was desperate. I had to get there, fast.

In a flash of fear, I turned my board and started to race for the shore, kicking and paddling as hard as I could, trying to get out of that spot. But the shore wasn't close and I didn't know how much time I had.

Fear of the unknown was the worst fear I'd ever known. A million thoughts raced through my head. I remembered that most people who were attacked by a shark never see their attacker approaching.

I braced for the impact I hoped would never come. I didn't want to believe my worst nightmare was unfolding with no warning, in familiar water so close to home, on an ordinary day. Suddenly everything looked different. Fear burned through my body. My stomach tightened. My heartbeat quickened. My body tensed like a runner's before a race. Every muscle was alert. I felt the awful uncertainty. God, I prayed it wouldn't happen. To get away was my only hope.

"Help. . . Help me. . . ."

I screamed for help. My voice sounded thin, barely audible over the breaking waves. I shrieked with fear. But no one heard. Everyone else was completely unaware of what was happening.

I could see Sean standing on the beach fifty yards away. His calm movements contrasted with my tension. He threw his towel over his shoulder and for a moment I thought he stared out in my direction, but I knew he didn't understand. His face showed no sign of concern and he was well beyond shouting distance. I was totally on my own.

I didn't know if I could possibly get to shore. I tried to swim as fast as I could, but I anticipated the shark's return at any moment, yet not really knowing. I watched the water for any sign of movement; it was calm and flat. The ocean showed no sign of danger. A thin facet of light flashed in the water beneath me. The shadows were playing tricks on me.

Kicking with all my might, clasping my board with clenched hands, I raced to get away, moving, pushing, straining forward with every ounce of my energy. This was the most terrifying moment I had ever known, or would ever know, the moment of absolute intense dread when you face the most awful fear. Fear of the jaws. And fear of the jagged teeth.

I swam as hard and fast as I could, breathing heavily, heading in, terrified of what might happen next. I searched the water as I swam, watching for a fin slicing through the water. I saw nothing at all but I held myself ready. Echoes of a foghorn lingered in the air but offered no comfort. All other distractions faded. I was totally focused on getting away.

The ocean stretched before me, great in its depth, terrifying in its emptiness. The mood had changed. Here where I'd always felt so safe, I felt the cold dark water surrounding me. I was desperate to get to shore. Kicking with all my strength, trying to get away, I moved through the water as fast as I could. But not fast enough.

CHAOS STRIKES

"Imagine how you would feel if you knew a big white shark was hunting for food and you are its next meal."
—*KNBC News*, Los Angeles

The shark slammed into me full force from below in a violent explosion of power, like a freight train with a mouthful of razorblades. It plowed into me so hard and fast, my body heaved with the impact. With one formidable bite the shark had my leg and hip trapped in its jaws. It flipped me over and off my board, and pulled me underwater. In an instant I was helplessly submerged. I knew at once this was a great white shark; its power was unmistakable.

The attack was sharp, accurate, and crystalline in its precision. Even the shark's swift ascent from below did not disturb the surface of the water. Never was the dorsal fin visible from above. Instinctively, the shark tried to inflict a mortal wound with one deadly first bite. I felt the explosion of pain shoot through my body like being hit by a truck and stabbed by a hundred knives all at once.

The teeth popped through my skin, sliced through my flesh, and clamped onto my bone like a kitchen knife cutting into an apple. Pain flooded my body. The shark tightened its grip and dragged me down into dark water, carrying me further from the shore, into its world and away from my own. I was trapped in rows of razor-sharp teeth and tangled in watery trails of kelp. The jaws were clamped firmly onto my bone, not like the loose grip of someone grabbing me. The shark held tight and started to thrash, shaking me from side to side.

Under the surface the sea exploded in violence and confusion as the shark dragged me along, pulling on my leg, trying to tear me apart. The jaws engulfed my leg, tearing my flesh from my knee to my hip. For this huge creature, I was merely a mouthful.

Fear flashed through my mind as the teeth tore through my body. This was a battle for my life and I knew it. I had to fight back. But the shark was impervious to my efforts.

I felt the muscles of my leg twist. I knew exactly what was happening. The shark was trying to break my leg, trying to tear it away from the rest of my body. I couldn't let it rip off my leg. My mind stopped there and didn't process any further. I didn't want to think about what would happen next. I was determined not to let it take my leg. And not to let it drag me out to sea.

My heart pounded, the pain was unbearable. Underwater I couldn't scream or take a breath. I refused to think of what was happening to my leg. I had only one thought—to save my life.

Feeling helpless and upside down in a turbulent nightmare, I struggled beneath the surf, trying to get away. The huge form loomed over me, as big as a motorboat. Its body lashed from side to side, sweeping the water in all directions. The image was surreal and I was horrified.

The unforgiving jaws held tight, like the immutable weight of a boulder. The power and pain were unrelenting. I tried to get away, pushing and pulling, but I couldn't pull free unless the shark chose to release me. Images of my family came to mind – my brothers, Michael and Eric, and my parents. I remembered how much I loved them.

Teeth and violence assaulted me. The ocean became a blur as the shark pulled me along through the water. I was afraid my leg would break like a twig. Churning water and sand engulfed me. The teeth tore deeper and the swirling water turned red. The shark gave no sign of retreat. Its grip never weakened. Instinctively the shark fought like the great predator it was. Its mastery was beyond question.

The shark arched over me, dragging me further into its own deep water. Its jaws encompassed my leg, pushing, pulling, and tearing at my hip, forcing the razor-sharp teeth deeper. Somehow I managed to stay calm, but I was desperate to get away.

My anger grew as I realized what was happening. Now I was mad at the shark and determined not to give up. The surge of anger empowered me. This was not how I wanted my life to end. I let go of fear and doubt and set my goal to live. Survival was more about determination than power.

I couldn't see its eyes or punch its nose because the shark's jaws were clamped onto my leg, low and out of reach. Thankfully I couldn't see the teeth tearing into my leg. With my thigh in its mouth, I was dragging along beside the shark two or three feet behind its head. With the poor visibility and the swirling sand and water, I could see only the side of the shark's body, a dark grey outline before me.

I reached out to grab the shark, trying to hold on, to gain some control. Maybe if I could stay with it, the shark wouldn't swim away with my leg in its mouth. But I couldn't get my arms around it. The shark was too big. Its massive girth stunned me. I was small by comparison, caught by its monumental strength, racing against time, struggling to get away.

My heart beat faster and I searched for a way to fight back. It was not my life that flashed before me, or a white light. What flashed before me was the challenge to fight. Through the turmoil of sand and water, I saw the shark's gills on the side of its body, just behind its head. Without thinking, I let my instincts take over. Maybe all those years of wrestling with my brothers on the living room floor were finally paying off. Instinctively, I knew what to do.

I grabbed hold of the gills with both hands like grabbing the handlebars on a bike. The huge slits were as wide as my hand. I pulled as hard as I could, grasping at my only hope to survive. My hands penetrated the rough outer skin and I could feel the sharp cartilage inside. Holding onto the gills was my chance to stay with the shark and save my leg.

Gripping the gills connected me to this huge creature and for a time I was one with the shark. I could no longer tell the difference between the shark and me. The shark's muscular body was rough and firm. I could feel its tremendous strength and power. The gills were solid, impervious to my grip. My efforts drew me closer to the shark's

massive body as I struggled to hold on. Caught in the jaws
of one of the greatest forces of nature, I realized the enor-
mity of my attacker.

Then, suddenly the jaws released me. For some
unknown reason, the shark let me go. The jaws set me
free and I bolted to the surface, flashing into the daylight
gasping for air. For this golden moment I felt triumphant.
Suddenly, I had a chance to get away. Getting to shore
alive was my only thought.

The shark was gone, or perhaps circling back for
another try. I searched the water, dreading the sight of a
fin. I sucked in a deep breath of air and found renewed
strength to keep going. My adrenaline kicked in and the
shore came into focus. A second ago, I was fighting for my
life; now the shark was giving me a second chance.

I had to get away before it came back. Having crossed
one threshold, my ordeal continued. I knew I was not safe.
As long as I was in the water I was still in the shark's territory. The shark had let me go, and there was no time to
question why. At least for the moment the shark was gone.
But I was afraid it would hit me again without warning.

OUT OF THE JAWS?

"Courage is like a kite,
an opposing wind raises it higher."
—Anonymous

The shark retreated for a time, leaving me on the edge of exhaustion. I was out of the jaws, but I expected it to come back. My journey to safety had only begun. Cool air jolted my awareness. My muscles tensed to flee and my eyes burned with salt and sand. Pain overshadowed every other sensation.

The pain told me my leg was still attached to the rest of me but I didn't look down; I didn't have time. I could feel it, but I couldn't move it. Worst of all, I thought I might lose it. I didn't know how bad it was. I was afraid it was only hanging by a thread. The cold water did nothing to numb the pain, the most severe pain I could ever imagine.

I scanned the surface of the dark empty water. The shark had vanished as suddenly as it first appeared. A cold shiver swept through me. I prayed the shark would leave me alone.

Gulls soared above, screeching a loud warning. My anger flared and I refused to heed their cries. "No, I will not give up. And I WILL get myself back to shore."

I found my board floating on the surface, the leash still tangled around me. I needed it to keep me afloat and help me swim. I yanked the cord and it slid across the water toward me. This single motion signaled hope; with my board came the chance to survive.

I pulled myself onto the board and it tipped from side to side in the choppy water. Holding onto it with shaky arms, I struggled to gain stability. The board wobbled beneath me. I felt unsteady and vulnerable with my leg bleeding and dangling as I floated precariously on top of the water still fifty yards from shore.

Injured and winded, I paddled frantically with my torn leg hanging at my side. Fear propelled me forward, pulling, groping, straining, clawing the choppy water with long strokes. The heavy, flat ocean slowed my every movement. I couldn't get going fast enough. The shore looked reachable, but not close. I had to make it. Nothing else mattered. Escape was my only thought. I was desperate to avoid what I dreaded was coming. Waves of fear swept over me. The ocean had become frightening and unfamiliar.

I watched the wavering line between sea and sky. Nothing appeared. Never did a dorsal fin disturb the surface of the water. For now, the ocean hid its secrets beneath its surface. And yet I knew the shark was still out here.

I struggled through the water with my arms and one good leg, using all my energy, trying to endure the pain, determined to save my life. My injured leg dangled, completely useless. I feared the shark would smell blood and come back. I looked to the beach, searching for safety, trying to reassure myself that I had a chance to make it. I needed help. I prayed for a wave to give my board a push and carry me in but the water was flat.

No one saw my distress; I was out there alone. I couldn't go fast enough. I felt the pull of the mighty ocean resisting and clinging to me. I pulled harder, struggling through dark, scary water. Each time I reached into the water to take another stroke, I was terrified.

"H-e-l-p."

The sound of my voice came from somewhere deep inside me, like the low, mournful sound of a wounded animal. Heads turned in my direction; faces looked puzzled, oblivious to what was happening. No one noticed how I was struggling to stay afloat or how the water was growing red around me. They didn't know I needed help.

"Help. I'm serious. I really need help."

I screamed with all my strength but I didn't yell "shark," because no one would come if they knew there was a shark out there. My words echoed across the water, lost in the thundering surf. No swimmers came and no one rushed out from the beach. It was up to me to save myself.

My arms slapped the water, each effort more intense, trying to get to shore. My strokes were ragged as I lurched forward across the empty expanse of ocean. *Keep heading in. Don't look back.* I didn't want to be there when the shark circled back. This was life or death and I knew it. I was determined to keep going.

I kept paddling toward the beach, closer to people who could help, trying to cross the thin line from danger to safety. Panic gripped every muscle as I watched the shore become closer. I heard the echo of the Stinson Beach whistle sounding the hour. The steady sound of the whistle urged me forward. Fog crossed the sky drifting over the beach. The coastline stretched before me; sheer willpower kept me going.

"Help." My voice grew louder and more guttural.

Finally reaching knee-deep water I collapsed. I dropped my head onto my board and sank onto my elbows in the shallow water. Waves rolled over my shoulders as I floated on my board. I was still overwhelmed with fear, hardly moving, exhausted and unable to stand. Somehow I'd made it to shore. Now that I was safe, I could admit my helplessness against the shark. I felt a momentary sense of victory until the pain overwhelmed me. I'd endured an ordeal beyond anything I could have imagined.

A teenage boy with a boogie board noticed me. He ran and splashed toward me in the shallow surf and tried to steady me in the water. He looked puzzled when he saw my leg and the red-orange water that swirled around us.

"What happened?"

"A shark." My voice was raspy and weak. I saw his expression change immediately.

"Here, let me help you."

The boy grabbed my arms and pulled me closer to shore. Unrelenting waves battered us in the shallow water. I was relieved and thankful for the boy and for the greater spirit watching over me.

Then the boy's mom rushed over and I heard her shout, "Shark! Shark."

My relief at being near shore was mixed with embarrassment, kind of like falling off your bike and hoping no one notices. I wanted to pretend I wasn't hurt. But it was too late.

Sean ran across the sand, rushing to get to me. He pulled the towel from his shoulder and pressed it gently over my leg at the spot where blood was pouring out of my torn wetsuit. The water streamed red with blood as the next wave washed over me.

"Jonathan, are you okay?"

"I think I'm okay," I replied through ragged breaths.

"Don't worry, I see the lifeguards coming to help," he said. He tried to comfort me and the sound of his voice reassured me.

A woman dressed in a business suit rushed into the water without worrying about her clothes or her shoes. She tried to help me but she quickly realized how serious it was.

"Get some help over here, quick," she called.

Sirens screamed from the nearby Stinson Beach Fire Department. Oddly, thoughts of my childhood and my family came back to me. The murmur of voices on the beach reminded me of the safe world of my younger days. Memories floated up and swept across my mind. I thought of the summer days with my brothers at the little Tower Lakes beach where we had so much fun and we were always safe.

Pat, the lifeguard, sprinted across the beach and knelt beside me at the water's edge. He knew me from many days at the beach. I recognized his red lifeguard trunks and his t-shirt with the word "Guard." I'd seen him on the beach many times, too, and his presence reassured me. But I couldn't talk; the pain was becoming more unbearable every minute.

"Let's get you out of the water," he said. "The paramedics are on their way. I've called for a helicopter—it'll be here in twenty minutes. Can you hang on?"

"Okay," I groaned, "but I don't want to move."

People from the beach rushed over to help. Their faces couldn't hide their shock. Strong arms pulled me out of the water. They turned me gently onto my back. Pat directed the others to place two boogie boards end-to-end to create a makeshift stretcher.

"We'll carry you up onto the dry sand."

"Sure. Okay." I was relieved to be out of the water and too exhausted to help myself.

They lifted me onto the improvised stretcher and carried me up onto the beach. It hurt when they moved me, a piercing pain worse than anything I'd ever experienced. I tried to ignore the pain and the sound of the walkie-talkie scratching and blaring from the waist strap of one of the lifeguards. They lowered me carefully onto the dry sand. My body drooped heavily. Finally, I was safe on land. Out of the waters of the Red Triangle.

Steve, another lifeguard, drove along the length of the beach in the white patrol truck shouting through a megaphone, "Clear the water . . . shark attack. Everybody out of the water."

"Shark attack!" someone else screamed. Faceless voices called out, but I was not listening to them; I was trying to endure the overwhelming pain that burned through my body.

"Please give me something for the pain," I begged.

"Not until the paramedics arrive to check your vital signs."

"Why is it taking so long?"

"Just a few more minutes."

Pat stayed at my side and comforted me as we waited for the paramedics. I was relieved to hear sirens screaming closer and the sound of help arriving. I tried to concentrate, to stay calm and focused, to block out the pain. People rushed to the water's edge to look for some sign of the shark. Lifeguards repeated the warning up and down the beach. The danger of the Red Triangle was more real than ever.

The sudden attack brought strangers together on the beach. Onlookers gathered around me. I couldn't believe all the turmoil. Faces encircled me, visibly shaken when they saw my leg. Strangers looked down with kindness and offered to help but there was little anyone could do. The voices echoed with alarm and shock, wondering how this could happen on a summer afternoon at Stinson Beach.

I heard people telling me I was brave and courageous. I let the words wash over me. Lying on the sand, unable to move, I felt small and helpless compared to the incredible power of the shark.

"Sean, how bad does it look? Is my leg still attached?" I asked. I tried to raise myself up onto my elbows to look at my leg but Sean quickly covered my eyes with his hand and carefully eased me back down onto the sand. He didn't want me to see it.

"Jonathan, I can see the bone in your leg, and your kneecap is exposed. I'm sure it'll be okay but I don't want you to look." Sean sounded nervous. He stepped away, looking light-headed and pale. He sat on a log nearby with his head in his hands.

A man in shorts knelt in the sand next to me. "I'm a doctor. I'll try to help you," he said. Hearing his calm voice reassured me even though there was little anyone could do. More sirens erupted in deafening confusion and fear rang out on the beach. I closed my eyes to concentrate on getting through it. Pain burned, but I tried not to think about the pain or what had happened to my body. I wished I could sleep and forget about the shark but sleep was impossible. Patches of windblown fog swept across the sky above me.

A commotion erupted with ambulances and fire trucks arriving at the beach. An ambulance stopped at the edge of the sand and two paramedics jumped out. One of them opened a big first aid box, grabbed a pair of scissors, and started cutting off my wetsuit.

"Wait," I protested. "Can't you save my wetsuit? I might want to wear it again."

"We need to stabilize you and stop the bleeding," he replied. In spite of my protests he continued cutting. Someone tossed my shredded wetsuit into the back of a pickup truck that was parked on the sand nearby.

"Shark experts will want to study the bite marks and the shape of the jaws," he said. They covered me with a towel because I was left lying on the beach without a swimsuit or a wetsuit. At that point, I didn't care.

The paramedics checked my vital signs and made sure I was conscious. Their faces told me they'd never responded to a shark attack. They applied pressure to my leg, trying to stop the bleeding. I only wished the pain would stop.

"What's going to happen? Will I lose my leg?"

"Don't worry about that right now, just try to relax."

I couldn't relax. Everything hurt. It was worse than anything, but I tried to stay calm. My throat was parched from the salt water and the struggle.

Next the paramedics placed me onto a backboard and applied pressure to straighten my leg, a routine procedure with broken bones and the possibility of a neck injury. They began to tighten the straps on my leg but with no muscles or tendons to hold the bones of my leg together the pain became unbearable.

"Uhhh," I groaned in excruciating pain. "I'm a lifeguard, too, and I know I don't need the backboard." I continued to protest until they finally agreed and removed it.

A woman with a video camera was filming the scene on the beach. A man on a cell phone was talking to a local news station. "A helicopter has been dispatched to Stinson Beach where a shark has attacked a sixteen-year-old boy. The victim is seriously injured," I heard him say. Already news of the shark was spreading fast.

Random thoughts and images of the shark floated through my head as I tried to deal with the pain. I felt a sense of triumph because I'd made it back to shore alive, but not without cost. The ocean would never be the same for me. The hard, cold reality was, I felt sad. The ocean had betrayed my confidence in one swift, violent clash.

Unbelievable pain overshadowed all emotions. To keep the excruciating pain under control, I tried not to think about it. I tried to deny the pain, telling myself it didn't exist. Most of all, I tried not to think about the ocean or the shark.

I could see the oxygen mask and the green oxygen tank ready to go. But before the paramedics gave me oxygen, they wanted to ask me questions.

"What is your name . . . your age . . . who should we contact?" I was grateful for their help, but I really didn't want to talk to anyone.

"You can ask my friend Sean. He's right over there," I said.

"We need to talk to you, to make sure you remain conscious."

"Oh, that's it." I began to realize what was going on. They were trying to keep me awake.

"Please give me something for the pain," I begged. Every minute lying there on the beach was torture.

"Yes, just a few more minutes," they said. I closed my eyes and waited, but every minute seemed like forever.

At last the sleek red helicopter appeared out of nowhere and circled the beach. Its blades pounded the air, blowing sand in every direction. With the rush of wind and sand everything became a blur. The deafening noise hurt my ears. My heart pounded in my chest. Never would this day seem other than a confused dream.

Pat directed the pilot where to land and the helicopter landed right on target. Its huge rotors slowed and the engines whined down to a dull roar. The paramedics lifted me onto a stretcher and rushed me across the sand. Within minutes I was lying flat inside the helicopter and the door slammed. The huge blades began to turn again and the helicopter lifted off. The air rescue was underway.

The chopper lifted off and banked over the beach. It turned sharply inland and skimmed high above the trees. Lying flat on my back, I couldn't see the beach beneath us but I could imagine the wide ocean that stretched beyond the shore and the shark still swimming out there. The pilot swept across San Francisco Bay, rushing me to a trauma center in Walnut Creek in the East Bay.

Inside the helicopter, I stared up at the geometric pattern in the dull grey ceiling directly above me. An oxygen tank, instruments, and medical equipment surrounded me in the tiny cabin. The emergency nurse sat close to me at my head.

I wished I could see my family: Mom and Dad, Michael and Eric, to tell them what had happened, but I was worried I might upset them. I didn't want to cause them too much trouble. I wondered what they'd say when they heard about the shark.

"I start school tomorrow," I said to the nurse who leaned over me. "Do you think I'll be able to go?"

"I guess we'll see," she said, smiling at my question as she continued checking and monitoring everything.

"You're a lucky kid," the pilot said to me above the noise of the engine. "I've seen lots of accidents, but never a shark attack. That shark could've torn your leg off."

I didn't feel lucky, but I knew he was right. I'd wait to hear what the doctors would say about my injuries. My mind raced with crazy thoughts. I hoped the helicopter wouldn't be too expensive. I wondered if our insurance would pay for it. Most of all, I was worried about my leg, and whether the doctors would be able to save whatever was left of it.

"We're heading for John Muir Trauma Center," the pilot informed me.

"But wait, I'm a member of Kaiser. I don't know if my insurance will cover it."

"Don't worry about that. It's the designated trauma center for Stinson Beach, the best trauma center in the

Bay area, with state-of-the-art medical equipment and a team of doctors waiting for you. That's what's most important right now."

My body felt as if it was on fire. My leg and hip were slashed open; I was exhausted and consumed by the ordeal. I tried to remain calm while enduring the raging pain. I hoped the ride to the hospital wouldn't take long.

"Just rest now," the nurse said. She gave me an injection of something and said it was morphine for the pain. I didn't want anything so strong, but there was no other way. I knew I was in good hands now. Fatigue settled over me and I closed my eyes for some unknown length of time. At least for a time I was relieved of the pain and away from the Red Triangle.

REPAIR AT THE
HOSPITAL

"Blood in the water . . .
Teen's lesson: If a shark bites,
don't forget to fight back."
—*San Francisco Examiner*

I awoke to the resurgence of pain splitting my leg. The helicopter floated to a landing on the helipad at John Muir Medical Center, the trauma center located across the Bay in Walnut Creek, California. The sound of churning blades faded away quickly as the engines whined to a stop. They rushed me inside without wasting a moment. Bright lights flooded the big emergency room and a team of doctors waited for me, ready to begin.

"I'm Doctor Wong, head of the trauma team. I'll be helping you," one of the doctors said. I was relieved to be in good hands.

"I'm the conductor of the symphony," Dr. Wong continued. "I'll be coordinating all the members of the medical team to give you the best possible care. We'll get some information from you before we begin. I'm pleased you're able to remain so calm."

He asked my name and phone number and told me the surgery was about to begin. He turned to his team. "Time is critical; he's still bleeding," he said to the others.

Five doctors, experts and specialists in their fields, huddled around, checking me. Their faces were covered with surgical masks but I could see kindness in their eyes. I listened to their voices and the sounds of the hospital around me.

The repair of my leg, as well as my life, was now in the hands of the doctors. They worked efficiently and seriously as they evaluated my condition and coordinated my treatment. Their immediate concern was how much blood I'd lost and whether I'd need a transfusion. I teetered between worlds, feeling light-headed as they examined the exposed muscles and bones of my torn leg. I hoped they could repair the damage done by the shark.

A lady dressed in pink stepped closer to me and dialed a portable phone. "We need to call your mother to tell her you're here," she said softly. I imagined the telephone ringing at home in Lucas Valley so many miles away across the Bay. She said hello to someone at the other end of the phone, talked for a minute, and then handed me the phone.

"Your mother would like to hear your voice," she said.

"Hello," I said. "Mom? Yes, I'm okay, but my leg really hurts."

My mother sounded breathless on the other end of the phone. The clear, steady sound of my own voice surprised me, but I didn't want to say too much; I didn't want

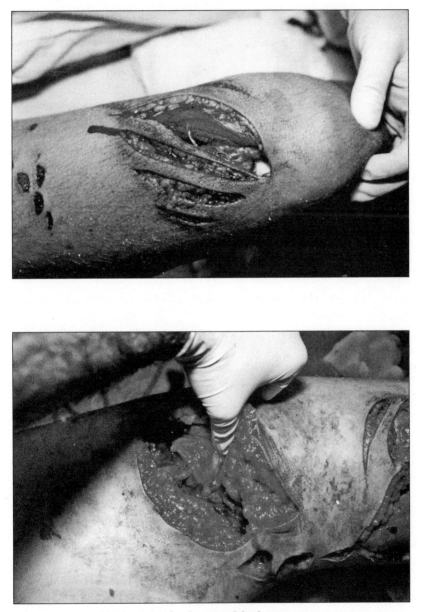

My leg, at the hospital before surgery

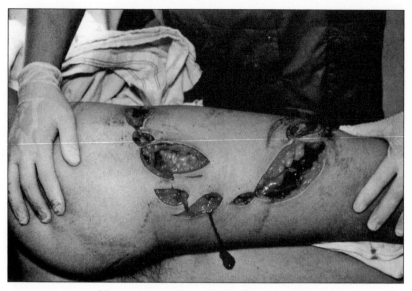

More views of my leg before surgery

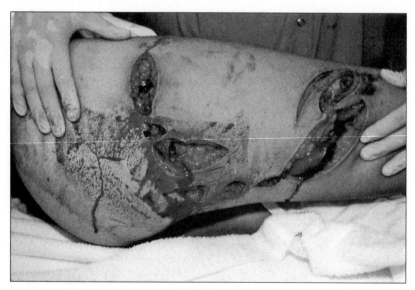

Photos courtesy of Dr. Homayoun Attaran, MD

to worry her. A phone call from the hospital was one that every mother would dread, her child in crisis. I was sure she'd never imagined that a great white shark, the mightiest predator of the ocean, would attack me. I resisted telling her how awful the shark attack really was, or how badly my leg was torn.

"Mom, I just really want to see you and Dad and Michael and Eric. When can you come?"

"I'm rushing to the hospital right now with Michael and Eric," she said. "I'll call Dad and he'll come from his office in San Francisco. We'll all be there as fast as we can. I love you, Jonathan."

The sound of her voice comforted me. But, after only these few words, our conversation ended.

I focused again on what was happening around me in the hospital. I wondered if the doctors would be able to save my leg. I was worried they might have to amputate it but I didn't want to ask. With this thought in my mind, I was wheeled into a nearby surgery room.

"We're taking you into surgery now. You'll be asleep for a while," Dr. Wong said. That was the last I remembered for a long time.

Hours later I opened my eyes in the dim light of the recovery room. I had no idea where I was. The bed, the room, and the sounds were unfamiliar to me. Then I saw my family, my mom, my dad, Michael, and Eric gathered around me. As I looked up into their faces, my eyes moving from one to the next, I could see their love and their range of emotions—they were anxious, proud, worried, and relieved. Mom had tears in her eyes, but we all probably did at that moment. I was thankful to see them and grateful to be alive. Already the shark had given me an even greater appreciation for my life and my family around me.

I wanted to sleep and forget everything that had happened, but I couldn't forget the pain that throbbed in my leg. I faded in and out until Dad's voice finally brought me out of my fatigue. I opened my eyes and I tried to make sense of my surroundings.

"Jonathan, you're at the hospital in Walnut Creek. You just had a long operation to patch up your leg."

Although it seemed like only minutes, Dad said I'd been in surgery for nearly eight hours. The repair had taken many hours longer than the doctors expected and the team had worked steadily into the night. Things were starting to make sense now that I was fully awake. Doctors and nurses hovered over me, showing their concern.

"What time is it?" I asked.

"Nearly midnight."

"I guess I survived the shark but I can't believe it really happened. Sorry if I worried you."

"Jonathan, you did a good job out there in the water, getting yourself back to shore. We're really proud of you. You stayed calm and did all the right things," Dad said.

"Jonathan, I'm so relieved to see you," Mom said. "What can I do to make you more comfortable?"

"Just being here with me is good," I replied.

"You've had hundreds of stitches," the doctor said. "At about two hundred stitches we stopped counting. We were able to save your leg, but we're not certain what the lasting effects might be."

I looked down at my leg. It was a maze of staples, stitches, plastic tubes, and bandages, and an array of monitors and blinking lights flashed at my side. Dad stepped aside to talk to the doctors about details of the surgery and what they did to fix my leg. I could hear him asking what would happen next.

Michael seemed uncharacteristically quiet while he looked at all the electronics and medical equipment and gauges hooked up to me. Michael always studied things and noticed every detail. I could tell he was trying to figure out how everything worked.

"This hospital has all the latest equipment," he said. "I wonder how long you'll have to stay hooked up?"

"I don't know, but it's okay for now."

"Jonathan, I wish we could go out and hunt that shark and eat it for dinner," Michael said with a smile.

"I know you're kidding, Michael, but I guess it's a good thing we don't have a boat. Anyway, thanks for wanting to stand up for me."

Eric looked concerned and I knew he was worried about me. He gave me a hug and placed a soft teddy bear next to my pillow. "We bought this for you in the gift shop downstairs while we waited all those hours." He looked at my leg covered in bandages, tubes, and staples. A shark attack was shocking and scary when it happened to your big brother, the one you'd always looked up to. Now he was the strong one.

"Good job, Jonathan, you beat the shark," Eric said, reaching out to hold my hand. Taking my hand, he was comforting me and I think I was comforting him, too.

Mom brushed away the grains of sand still clinging to my salty face, my hair, and even inside my ears. The violence of my struggle was still evident, even after all these hours of surgery. She checked my feet to make sure they were warm. I was glad both of my feet were still there and her warm hands felt good. She gave me a hug, trying not to bump my leg or my battered body. Her face showed how relieved she was and I could tell she'd been crying.

"You don't need to cry any more, Mom. I'm going to be okay."

"Yes, you're doing fine," she smiled.

Our neighbor Ken surprised us all when he appeared in the doorway of the recovery room with a big smile as always.

"How did you know I was in the hospital?" I asked.

"I saw your shark story on the evening news. When I saw your mom and your brothers on TV at the emergency room entrance, I rushed to the hospital to check up on all of you. When these things happen, you don't wait to ask questions, you just show up."

"I wasn't expecting to get this much attention," I said.

"Your shark attack is all over the news. You're famous now, Jonathan. And I'm glad you're okay." Ken's familiar chuckle lit up the room and his presence gave us the support we needed.

Sean had been standing back, waiting for a chance to say hello. Finally he stepped closer to the bed to talk to me. He looked tired and anxious after our long day at the beach. I could tell he was shaken by everything he'd seen.

"Jonathan, are you doing okay? I feel awful, seeing you like this, all torn apart and stitched together. I saw your leg when you were lying there on the beach. It was awful," he said. And then he paused, as if he wasn't sure how to continue.

"Don't worry, Sean," I said. "I know there was nothing you could have done," I replied. I was reading his thoughts, thinking he felt bad because he'd gone back to the beach without me.

"I felt so helpless. I wish I could have helped you more," he said.

"It wasn't your fault. No one expected a shark."

"My mom and I drove back out to Stinson late this afternoon to pick up your car from the parking lot and all your stuff."

"Thanks, I'd forgotten about everything I left out there at the beach."

"I picked up your board too; it has a few bites in it. The shark experts took your wetsuit. They want to study the teeth marks to confirm what kind of shark it was."

Sean's mother, Connie, was there too. She put her arm around my mother to comfort her. "Are you doing okay?" she asked my mom.

"Yes, I think so," Mom said. But her voice sounded tentative.

"I think we'll head home now," Connie said. "It's getting late, you should all try to get some rest, too."

"Jonathan, in a few minutes, we'll take you to a room upstairs where you can sleep," the nurse said. "You've been through a lot,"

"That sounds good, I've never been so exhausted."

"Just rest now," she said.

The familiar voices of my family became a soft murmur as I faded in and out of sleep and pain. My parents continued to talk to the doctors and I was confident they'd be strong advocates, making sure everything possible was done to help me. My brothers and my parents stayed close to me, supporting and encouraging me. I was thankful to have my family around me; I didn't think I could get through the pain and uncertainty without them. I felt confident with their love and support. I didn't need to worry. I was finally safe.

I opened my eyes long enough to realize the nurse was wheeling me through a wide hospital corridor and into the elevator to a room upstairs. My family was right there, too. The motion of the bed felt like waves and I was floating in the ocean again. I tried to erase the images of the shark, but the shark had become an indelible part of me, redefining me and redirecting my life in ways I could not yet imagine.

I was proud because I'd fought back and survived. I had done my best against incredible odds and somehow, for whatever reason, my instincts and my refusal to give up had triumphed. The shark had let me go. Maybe the shark didn't like the taste of me. Maybe I cut off its air supply. Or perhaps there was some greater reason why I survived; I'd never know.

My hospital room was calm, but the turmoil inside my head continued with images and frightening dreams. I could still see the beach and the shark in the shadows of my mind. I tried to sleep but I couldn't forget that day. I struggled with the aftermath of pain and fear. I could still see everything clearly, as if watching a movie that kept replaying. Gradually, the dream slipped away but I slept badly, jolting in sudden pain and wakefulness.

Late that night, after everyone else had left, Mom sat beside my hospital bed. She rubbed my forehead and talked to me in the darkness.

"Jonathan, I'm so thankful you're alive . . . I couldn't possibly bear to lose you. You know I could not live without you."

"Thanks, Mom. I'm thankful to be here with you."

I could see a tear in her eye and we each knew how close we came to losing each other.

"Mom?"

"Yes?"

"You're staying all night with me, aren't you?"

"Yes, I wouldn't leave for anything."

"Thanks, Mom." Finally I drifted off into a deep and restless sleep until daylight.

Thursday, August 27, 1998
John Muir Trauma Center

The morning after my attack, I awoke to see Mom, Dad, Michael, and Eric already gathered at my bedside bright and early. I was sure they hadn't been at home long enough to get any sleep. Team Kathrein was here to support me. I didn't know what I'd do without them.

From the moment I awoke the pain was unbearable, like knives stabbing me everywhere. My head throbbed with every beat of my heart. Every small movement sent stabs of pain through my limbs. The pain came in waves, peaking into sharp arcs and then flowing outward through every part of my body. Pain medicine didn't seem to touch it, and besides that, I didn't like the side effects of heavy drugs. In addition to the pain, a burning thirst enveloped me. My throat was parched and dry. Mom was always ready with the glass of water and a straw, but as much as I

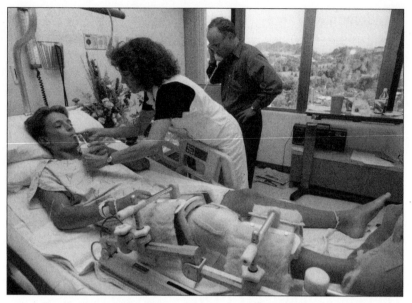

*In the hospital—Mom helping with a drink of water
and Dad on the phone*

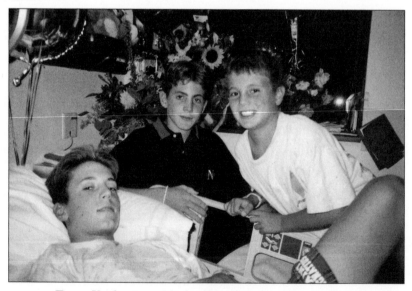

Team Kathrein—Michael and Eric at my bedside

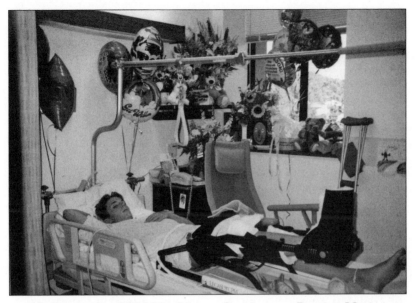

My leg in the CPM Machine—Continuous Passive Motion

drank, I couldn't seem to get enough. The doctors said the intense thirst was due to the extreme loss of blood from my injuries. My entire body felt as if I'd been through a battle. I struggled to stay in control.

My hospital room was a hub of activity with a seemingly endless stream of doctors and nurses rushing in and out, but the pain did not subside. Hour to hour I tried to get through it. Antibiotics and fluids dripped into my body and the nurses gave me pain medication when I needed it but it didn't really touch the pain. Specialists in every field were called in to consult. They spoke in medical terms I'd never heard, describing muscles, bones, tendons, skin grafts, and follow-up procedures. I felt their lingering concern about how everything would heal. The doctors weren't sure yet, nor was I.

My leg was a puzzle of black threads tracing irregular lines and stitches surrounding tiny patches of skin. My knee was red and puffy, and my leg was swollen to well beyond its normal size. I couldn't move my right leg at all. It looked red and inflamed with tubes, drains, staples, and stitches everywhere.

A special device arrived in my hospital room. An orthopedic technician placed the cumbersome machine on top of my bed, plugged it in, and strapped it to my leg. It kept my leg moving and flexing at the knee. The movement would prevent the scar tissue from tightening as it healed and rendered the joint immobile, limiting my range of motion. At first, even the smallest movement was painful but the doctor insisted it was important for my recovery. I endured it because I wanted to regain the full use of my leg.

A team of doctors encircled my bed. They examined my leg and observed the results of the previous night's surgery. The orthopedic surgeon spoke first. "The cuts in your leg and hip made by the shark's teeth were so deep, it looked like a chainsaw accident," he said. "I repaired your knee and reattached the kneecap and patella tendon, with a screw in the bone to secure the sutures. It's a strong repair; don't worry about it breaking when you move your leg. The suture material I used is strong enough to pull a truck out of a ditch." He smiled proudly, but I knew it would be a while before I'd be ready to test it.

"The impact from the jaws of the shark damaged the cartilage of your knee, much like the impact of a fall. You might expect to have some weakness and you might never be able to run, or lift your leg to the side," he said.

I heard what he was saying but I knew I wouldn't be satisfied with those limitations. I was determined to achieve more than that, but it would take hard work.

The plastic surgeon examined the stitches he'd used to reconnect and repair the skin. There were some small patches of skin he hoped would have sufficient blood flow to heal. His stitches were tiny and his work was meticulous.

"There are many more layers of stitches inside," he said. "The shark's teeth were so sharp they severed your muscles and tendons all the way down to the bone. I could feel a chip in your femur when I ran my hand along the bone on the inside of your leg. I used layers of delicate stitches to reconnect muscles and veins deep inside your leg. Some of the veins I stitched were as small as this little red coffee stirrer."

"Really?"

"I trimmed the ragged edges of flesh and pulled your skin tight to cover a couple of places where the shark swam away with a piece of your muscle in its mouth."

An infectious disease specialist told me there was still a danger of infection from the mouth of the shark. "We don't really know for sure what bacteria might have been in the mouth of the shark, in the sand, or even in the ocean. Even one grain of sand could cause an infection inside your leg. We used many liters of water under pressure to flush out every grain of sand that was inside your leg." He prescribed a range of antibiotics to be administered intravenously for the next two weeks and said I would be monitored closely for infection. The first few days would be critical and he cautioned us to watch for signs of redness and warmth that might indicate an infection. As far as I could tell, my leg already looked red and warm and swollen anyway.

"The teeth of the shark missed your femoral artery by only a centimeter," the surgeon said. "You're one of the unluckiest and luckiest people I know. Had the shark bitten one centimeter to the left, the teeth would have severed your artery and you would never have lived to swim to shore."

One tiny centimeter—the difference between life and death. Now I knew I had angels watching over me. I was lucky to be alive.

Pulsing monitors marked time as the hours passed in the hospital and I drifted in and out of sleep. Struggling with the pain was a constant challenge. I tried not to rely too much on pain medication; I preferred to use breathing techniques, but at times the pain was overwhelming and I needed the medicine.

Mom stayed at the hospital day and night, ready to help if I awoke with pain or dreams. Dad, Michael, and Eric stayed at my bedside for hours on end. We all laughed at their story about the breakfast Dad cooked for them at home now that Mom was at the hospital with me.

"Dad's oatmeal made with protein powder was so thick the spoon stood straight up in the bowl," Michael said. The oatmeal story became a classic family joke.

Most important to me was to know I could depend on them to help me get through anything. We were a family, ready to help each other.

Tracy, the hospital spokesperson, came to my room to tell us she had issued a press release in response to all the calls she was receiving from reporters and newspapers:

The sixteen-year-old shark attack victim is in critical but stable condition, with trauma to the major muscles and tendons of his leg from his knee to his hip. He faces a lengthy rehabilitation period.

That afternoon, the August sun scorched the golden hills outside my hospital window. Eric and Michael leaned on their elbows looking out the window, watching the hospital parking lot below.

"You should see all the news vans and TV satellite trucks outside," Eric said, looking out my hospital window.

"The parking lot is crowded with black SUV's and reporters with microphones and cameras waiting by the hospital door," Michael said. "They want to talk to you, Jonathan."

Dad turned on the TV in my hospital room. My shark attack was news on every channel, but the reports were brief and lacking detail. Photos of Stinson Beach showed curious onlookers and reporters staring out at the water, but no one saw any signs of the shark. Surfers and swimmers stayed out of the water. The beach was to remain closed for the rest of the week.

Reporters were eager for more. Television crews and reporters converged outside the hospital. The phone beside my hospital bed rang nonstop with calls from well-wishers and reporters wanting to ask me questions. Nurses delivered stacks of phone messages. Phone slips and newspapers piled up next to my bed. I was in too much pain to think about anything.

MEDIA FRENZY

"Our top story . . .
A sixteen-year-old shark attack victim is
lucky to be alive . . . Experts say the shark was
a great white . . . Probably out for a meal."
—Marc Brown, *ABC 7*
Eyewitness News, Los Angeles

The morning headlines were sensational, with stories entitled "Blood in the Water" and "Shark Attack at Stinson."
Sean's photo was on the front page of the *Marin Independent
Journal*. He looked expressionless and pale, standing on the
beach and holding his board after the attack.

Suddenly the shark, not just any shark, but a great
white shark, was the center of news. Reporters hoped to
capitalize on the story of the shark at Stinson Beach. They
wanted to ask me lots of questions. People were eager
to know more. There hadn't been a local shark attack in
recent memory. Even the locals had forgotten how the Red
Triangle got its name. Now the meaning was brutally clear.
Stinson Beach had achieved the ultimate reputation as a
shark-attack beach.

A media frenzy developed at the hospital and reporters moved in like the sharks they sought to portray. Satellite trucks from Fox News, CNN, Extra, CBS, and NBC hovered outside the hospital. Technicians waited for word that a live feed could begin. Television news anchors wanted to interview me for the evening news.

I was suddenly thrust into the spotlight. Everyone wanted to hear the details of my story. The phone rang with people asking questions, "Did it hurt? Were you scared? How many stitches? Will you go back in the water?" I had never expected to be in the middle of such a whirlwind of attention.

"Is this really news, Dad?" I asked.

"Of course it is. People want to hear how you fought the shark. They wonder if it will ever be safe to enter the water at Stinson again. They want to know how you survived."

"I can't talk to anyone right now. The pain is too intense." I couldn't think of anything but my throbbing leg.

But then I looked up from my hospital bed and I saw my wetsuit on television. An expert was holding my wetsuit by its torn leg and showing it for the camera. And then he carelessly tossed it aside.

"Hey, that's my wetsuit. They took it before I had a chance to even look at it." I was offended that my wetsuit had become a news item, out of my control. To me it was an important part of my survival, almost like a badge of courage.

The expert on TV was pointing out each tooth mark, explaining that the size of the teeth and the shape of the jaw indicated the predator was a great white shark. He explained

that the great white shark has rows of broad teeth with serrated edges sharp enough to cut through the tough hide of a
seal or take a chunk from a whale. The shark then leaves its
victim to weaken or bleed to death.

"But in this instance the boy's buddies helped him
to shore before the shark came back. That's what saved
his life."

"No," I bristled at this misinformation. "My buddies
did not help me. I saved myself."

By now I was not thinking of the pain anymore. I
wanted to tell my story and get it straight.

"The reporters are still waiting to talk to you," Dad
said. "Shall I send them away?"

"No, I want to talk to them. This won't be news
tomorrow."

Less than twenty-four hours after the attack, hardly
pausing to catch my breath, I felt strong enough to talk.
Hospital officials gave reporters the okay to enter my
room for an interview at my bedside. TV crews flocked
into my hospital room with cameras, microphones, lights,
and cords. It looked like a presidential press conference
was ready to begin. Nurses and doctors crowded in to lis-
ten. The questions began and my mind returned to that
day. This was the first I'd talked about it or described the
attack. Even my family hadn't heard all the details. The
room fell silent as I begin to speak . . .

"Yes, I noticed it was foggy, pelicans were diving, and
kelp was strewn everywhere on the beach. Visibility in the
ocean wasn't good."

"Yes, I was alone in the water when the shark bumped
me. It was only up to me to save myself and well, and

93

whoever watches over us. I had an added strength and fortitude that pushed me. It was the only point in my life when I was pushed, but not pushed by anyone other than myself so strongly to succeed. I did not have any earthly companion, coach, or parent to tell me what I needed to do. I knew what I had to do, and I survived.

"What was the next question? You asked if I saw its eyes? Hold on. I'll get to that in a minute. But there's a lot more to the story, and many more scary moments. Let me start from the beginning . . ."

My voice was steady as my mind turned back to the memories that were still so fresh. I told my story slowly, calmly, and methodically. Reporters listened in silence, taking notes and recording my account of pain and fear. My thoughts retraced the painful ordeal in slow motion, giving every detail of the attack. I could tell that many in the room did not know about the ocean and had never known real fear. Perhaps now they realized the true size and the incredible power of my attacker.

"Were you afraid?" someone asked.

"Of course I was afraid."

"Did it hurt?"

"Yes. The pain was unbelievable. You've seen photos of a shark attacking and tearing apart a seal . . . . Well, it was worse than you ever imagined a shark attack would be."

"What did you learn from your experience?" came another question.

"Having confronted life and death, I found a new understanding of my own humanity. I see life differently. I believe that each one of us finds an inner strength to handle whatever challenges we have to face."

"What advice would you give to anyone who might face a shark?"

"I would like others to know how I survived because I hope my experience might help someone else survive a shark attack. As with anything in life . . . keep trying and never give up."

Reporters were eager for more. They wanted quotes and sound bites that would portray the great white shark as a man-eater and a ruthless killing machine, but I didn't agree. I wanted to portray the shark as a peaceful yet powerful animal doing what it was supposed to do.

We decided to give Michael the job of "press secretary" to handle the continuing interview requests. He answered the phone beside my bed and took messages. He decided whom I would speak with, and he fended off the others. I wanted to do interviews that were factual and scientific, not sensational.

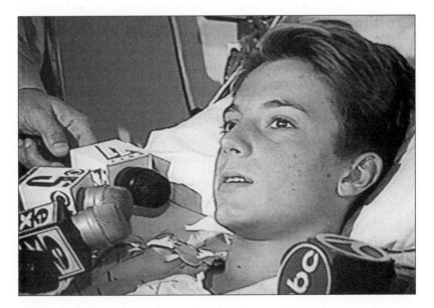

I heard Michael speaking to reporters outside my door, "Jonathan never worried about sharks," he said, "because we've never seen a shark at the beach." Reporters gave Michael's words a bold spin in the evening news. Headlines read, "My Brother Is Not Afraid of Sharks." Well, that wasn't exactly true.

I never expected the whirlwind of attention that enveloped me. News clips of my interview appeared on every television station throughout the Bay Area and beyond. Friends from Chicago called to say they'd read the story in the Chicago newspaper. Fox News sent a crew to my hospital room to set up a live appearance with Ross McGowan, the host of *Mornings On 2*. *Dateline NBC* filmed a family interview in my hospital room. They wanted to follow up with a continuation of the story at Stinson beach in six months. With all this interest, I'd gained a sort of local celebrity status. My fifteen minutes.

Mail arrived from around the world. I received letters decorated with hearts and flowers from girls in Germany who had seen my interviews and wanted to be pen pals. Relatives and friends across the country called from Iowa, Chicago, South Carolina, and Wisconsin. The cast from *Phantom of the Opera* sent an autographed poster and an invitation for my family and me to attend the show. The German television network ZDF offered to fly our family to Germany in December, all expenses paid, to appear on *People of the Year.* We agreed to fly to Cologne for the live appearance. But when someone on the staff of *The Oprah winfrey Show* called, I declined to be interviewed. I was already overwhelmed with so much going on in my life.

RECOVERY AND
HEALING

"We shine brightest when we treat each other with
respect and kindness, and by treating others well
we allow them to shine too."
—Jonathan Kathrein, *Don't Fear the Shark*

No one saw the shark anywhere near the beach during the
days following my attack. The lifeguards assumed it had
moved back out to sea. And yet the fascination did not
cease. People wanted to hear more about sharks, but much
of the available information only reinforced the shark's
image as a fearsome killer.

Ever since the publication of *Jaws* and the ensuing block-
buster movie based on the book, great white sharks attained an
almost mythical status as the ultimate creatures to be feared.
They were almost always described in superlative terms
as vicious hunters lurking at the beach. And yet questions
remained as to which stories were true and which were myths
fueled by fear. I became interested in knowing the answers.

After the publication of *Jaws*, Peter Benchley published a subsequent book in which he tried to redeem the

image of the shark he had so badly devastated. He saw the need to clarify that great white sharks were not the blood-thirsty manhunters portrayed in his first novel. In *Shark Trouble*, speaking about shark attacks, Benchley wrote, "Remember that no matter what you do, the odds are in your favor. Whether or not a person acts with vigilance and common sense, still the statistical chances of being set upon by a shark remain well within the comfort zone, somewhere between slim and none."

I learned that in reality, shark attacks are not the threat the media would have us believe. Many scientists work tirelessly to correct misconceptions about sharks and to save the dwindling shark populations from shark fin-ning, habitat destruction, overfishing, and becoming acci-dental by-catch. In truth, we humans are a much greater threat to sharks than they are to us.

Days in the hospital passed in a blur. I kept my sense of humor thanks to all the friends and visitors who stopped by and entertained me with shark jokes, telling me I must not have tasted very good because the shark spit me out, and saying the scar would be a babe magnet. Friends called me "shark man," "shark bait," and "gimpy," and I didn't mind. "I'll bet you got your best time swimming back to the beach that day," one of our neighbors from swim team joked. Yes, it was probably true.

The humor helped me get through the pain and helped keep my mind away from the memories. I tried to stay pos-itive to keep my thoughts from spiraling out of control. I wanted to learn more about sharks but the memories were scary and I didn't want to dwell on the shark attack.

Everyone who knew me seemed shocked by the shark

attack. My friend Kenny, who was also a surfer, showed up at the hospital with his mom and his brother, Scott.

"Jonathan," he said, "are you going to be okay? I mean your leg . . . is it still there?"

"Yes, I still have my leg. And I guess I'm lucky to be alive."

"I was driving home from Santa Cruz with my new board when I heard about the shark attack on the news. I never dreamed it would be you, Jonathan. You're the most cautious person I know."

"I still can't believe it myself."

"You did a good job, man. How did you fight a shark and get away?"

"I had to save myself. No one else was going to do it for me."

"Hey, you got to fly in a helicopter. How was the ride?" he asked with a smile.

"Painful," I said, trying not to remember.

"Do you think you'll go back in the water?"

"Yes, I hope so, but not for a long time."

The next day Pat Norton, the head lifeguard from Stinson Beach came to the hospital to visit me. He was dressed in his dark green park ranger uniform; so different from the shorts he often wore as a lifeguard at the beach. He sat on the edge of my bed and we talked about that day.

"I knew you'd want to have this back," Pat said, handing me the blue wetsuit they had taken from me on the beach. It was sealed in plastic and mounted on a board for display. I was happy to have it.

Flat on my back, I examined my torn wetsuit. The teeth marks showed the imprint of the jaws that held me as I fought for my life. Now the suit held unbelievable memories. It was an important reminder of my struggle and survival.

"Your wetsuit's been on exhibit at the Farallon Visitor Center at Crissy Field in San Francisco. Lots of folks were curious to see the marks from the teeth. Shark experts confirmed that the size and shape of the teeth marks indicate your attacker was a great white shark. But we already knew that."

"A shark at the beach was something I never expected," I said.

"Yes, shark attacks are very rare. I've never seen a shark attack at the beach. I've seen lots of injuries at the beach, but never anything like yours. The cuts in your leg were so massive and clean, it looked as if your leg was sliced by a razor or a really sharp knife."

"Thanks for helping me on the beach that day, and for coordinating the rescue," I said.

"I knew immediately it had to be a shark attack when I heard you calling for help from the water. I could hear the sound of terror in your voice. I knew the conditions were right for a shark to be close to shore."

Pat explained that "upwelling" is the phenomenon that brings nutrient-rich water, and sharks, closer to shore in late summer along the coast of Northern California. The upwelling current carries dense, cold water from a deep ocean trench offshore, bringing everything to life in the shallow waters of the coast and beaches. Shifting currents and weather patterns, the earth's rotation, and prevailing westerly winds drive surface waters offshore or parallel to the shore. Surface waters are replaced by deep, cold water that carries nutrients to the surface along the coast, bringing a food supply closer to shore than during the rest of the year.

This upwelling of nutrient-rich water brings everything to life along the coast. Blue whales, humpback whales, and Pacific white-sided dolphins feed on the abundant krill and schooling fish that aggregate offshore. Anchovies, mackerel, and baitfish move closer to shore, salmon swim through the protein-rich waters chasing the anchovies, seals feed on the salmon, and sharks, in turn, follow the seals. It's a remarkable phenomenon with lots of activity at the surface and under the water. The Pacific coast of Northern California becomes a rich feeding ground for fish, birds, seals, and sharks. Brown pelicans skim the water diving for fish and seagulls flutter above. Abundant food in the rich cold water draws everything closer. Sharks are right there, too.

I was amazed to hear Pat describe exactly the conditions I had observed that day at the beach. I remembered noticing how the ocean seemed full of activity, the water looked churned up, there was little visibility, fishing boats were close to the beach, and lots of seaweed from the ocean had washed up on shore. That day I didn't know these signs meant sharks were closer too.

"We rarely see sharks at the beach, except during the late summer months," Pat said.

"And I was in the middle of it all," I said.

"The minute I heard your cry, a deep guttural sound, I knew immediately a swimmer or surfer was in serious trouble. The sound was different from every other voice at the beach. From the tower I could easily spot you—every head in the water was turned in your direction. They heard you, but they didn't understand why you were calling for help. Your voice rang with the fear of life or death and I knew it had to be a shark. Before I left the tower to help you, I called for the paramedics and a helicopter."

Thoughts of Stinson Beach returned to me as I listened to Pat describe the events of that day. Without the help of a lifeguard, I knew my chances of surviving would have been greatly diminished. I thanked him again for helping me on the beach. I was certain we'd remain friends for a long time, connected by this unforgettable experience and our love of the ocean.

I knew that for Pat the ocean was much more than a job. It was a way of life. He took his responsibility seriously, reading the signs of the ocean and its ever-changing conditions. As a lifeguard and a Park Ranger for the Golden Gate National Recreation Area, he was ever watchful and ready to protect lives. Even more than that, like many surfers, he was a steward of the earth, helping to conserve and protect the ocean.

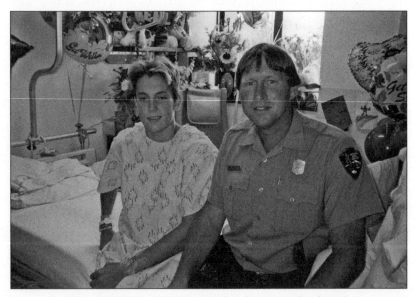

Pat, the lifeguard who helped me on the beach

The next morning I embarked on a serious routine of physical therapy that would continue for months. A physical therapist helped me practice walking down the hospital corridor with crutches and a leg brace. The therapist supported me with a heavy leather belt and Mom walked along beside me, providing frequent drinks of water. I returned to my hospital bed exhausted but happy to be getting stronger.

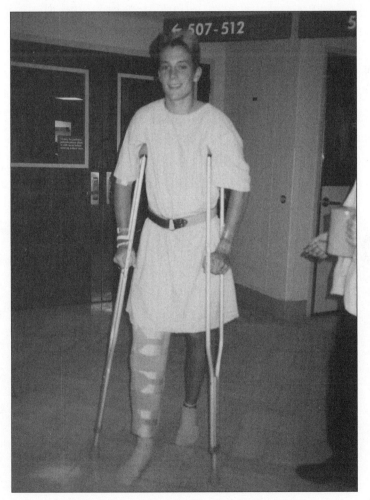

Practicing with crutches in the hospital

Family, friends, and visitors helped me get through the long and painful days of recovery. Their presence was the true meaning of friendship. Flowers, cards, and balloons filled my hospital room. Surfers from Hawaii sent a book called *Jaws Maui* with beautiful full-page photos signed by famous big-wave surfers. Shark music boxes, shark bathtub stoppers, shark swim goggles, shark stuffed animals, beanie baby sharks, shark neckties, and shark cartoons become treasured reminders of my survival.

A family friend sent a small plastic card laminated with my picture and a headline from the *San Francisco Chronicle*, "Help, I really need help." His note enclosed with it said, "Carry this card in your wallet as proof because in a few years no one's going to believe this story."

Many friends supported us, stopping by simply to be there with us. Their presence was a gift from the heart.

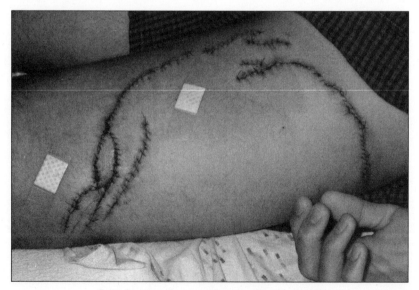

Stitches and wounds starting to heal

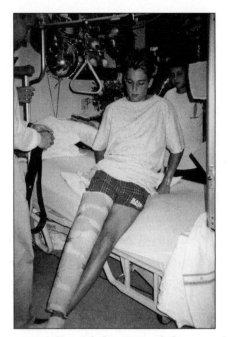

Learning to walk with leg immobilizer and crutches

Even beyond our family, my survival united our community. I learned how important it is to be present for others, to give of one's time, and to support those in need.

At Stinson Beach the National Park Service erected a large billboard at the entrance to the beach parking lot that read:

Swimmers and Waders
CAUTION
Shark Advisory -
Great white sharks live in these waters.
A shark attack occurred here in 6 feet of water.
Be aware of the potential for sharks close to shore,
along the entire length of the beach.

Another big sign, impossible to miss, was posted at the edge of the beach, "Beach closed to swimming and surfing." The sign alerted swimmers of my shark attack in six feet of water, a reminder that sharks could swim into shallow water and mistake humans for prey. Someone jokingly changed the sign at the edge of town to read, "Stinson Beach Population 632½."

Eric proudly told his friends at school, "My brother fought a great white shark and won." He drew cartoons for me with the shark complaining of sore gills saying, "That boy had a really strong grip on my gills."

Michael revealed his thoughts in an essay he wrote for school. "That one afternoon changed everything for me because of what happened to someone I love. I will think about the shark whenever I step into the ocean with my surfboard. The pain of this sudden and violent attack will remain with me forever. My brother had to stand in the face of death to teach me the value of life and I'm thankful I was able to learn. He could barely open his eyes, but he really opened mine."

I was touched by everyone's concern. Most of all, my family was my constant source of love and strength. They stayed with me, encouraged me, and helped me keep my sense of humor. In literal seconds our lives had changed forever. We all knew how much we valued each other and our awareness brought us closer in a way that would keep us together and strong.

My attack was shocking to our community too, perhaps because it was so close to home. It was the first shark attack ever recorded at Stinson Beach and the only attack along the North Coast in years. The previous attack two

years earlier, a fatal attack by a white shark on an abalone diver, had occurred many miles to the north along the
Mendocino coast, north of Point Reyes National Seashore.
My attack was the seventy-ninth shark attack in California
waters, and the tenth attack off the Coast of Marin County
since 1950.

As a result of my attack, awareness of sharks increased
along the North Coast and especially along the Red
Triangle. Coastal communities reported a swell of curious
onlookers at the beaches and fewer swimmers in the water.
More warning signs appeared.

Time magazine's cover story proclaimed the summer
of 2001 "The Summer of the Shark." The open jaws of a
great white shark engulfed the magazine cover. Stinson
Beach was closed for more than a week that summer after
lifeguards spotted a great white shark. The closure was
extended after a second shark was spotted in the same
area seventy five yards off the beach. And yet only five
people died from shark attacks worldwide that entire year.
Even with the relatively small number of attacks, news
surrounding sharks attracted worldwide attention.

The *Marin Independent Journal* declared Marin
County, California "Great White Central." A *Sports
Illustrated Adventure* magazine headline story entitled
"Feeding Frenzy" and proclaimed: "Goodbye and good
riddance to the summer of the Dull-Eyed Predator, the
silent voracious seeker of vulnerable flesh." A warning
sign on one beach seriously understated the risk of sharks:
"Warning: Dangerous Marine Life Has Been Spotted in
This Area." This sign appeared after ten shark attacks
occurred in a matter of ten days.

An increasing number of articles appeared in newspapers and magazines describing the Red Triangle, its location, and its dangers. Some of the articles were informative; others were merely sensational. Some scientists believe sharks are territorial, but no one knows exactly how large a shark's territory might be. Scientists agree that more great white sharks live in the Red Triangle than in any other place on earth.

Working with physical therapists in the hospital, I grew stronger, my leg was healing, and my condition improved each day. By the end of the week, I was desperate for sunshine and fresh air and eager to leave the hospital. The doctors were pleased with my progress and they agreed.

At home in Lucas Valley, the local press waited at our house to photograph my homecoming. Our neighbors had posted a long banner across the front of our house that read, "Home of the World Famous Shark Wrestler." My friends and teammates from the Lucas Valley Swim Team had signed it. We could all smile now; things were starting to look better. And yet each time I closed my eyes I could still remember the shark.

Home seemed familiar, yet somehow different. Everything in my life had changed. The world didn't seem as safe, but at the same time life was more wonderful than ever. I was happy and grateful for each day. I began to pay more attention to sunsets and the wind. I heard more songbirds and noticed clouds with silver linings. I had greater expectations, knowing that if I could escape the jaws of a great white shark, anything could be possible.

Messages continued to arrive from friends and neighbors offering their support. Many people helped us through

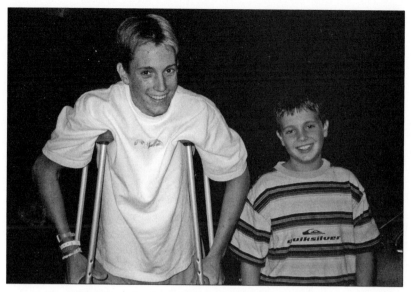

Leaving the hospital on crutches with Eric

Banner posted by our neighbors for my homecoming—"Home of the World Famous Shark Wrestler"

Returning to John Muir Medical Center with Mom for
follow-up appointments

Interview with Ross McGowan for Mornings on 2 *on Fox News*

this difficult and uncertain time. The kindness of friends amazed and comforted us.

We found an excellent sports medicine facility, called Active Care, known for sports and orthopedic rehabilitation. It wasn't close but it was highly recommended. Mom drove me into San Francisco for my physical therapy appointments and waited for me because I couldn't drive with my leg in a brace. Even though it was far from home, I wanted the best and most aggressive therapy for the best recovery. At each session I worked with a physical therapist named Coleman who coincidentally was also a graduate of St. Ignatius high school, a few years ahead of me. He structured a program that helped me target muscles that needed strengthening. We used a variety of exercise equipment as well as electronic biofeedback machines to evaluate muscle strength. We worked on strengthening and reeducating damaged muscles.

The exercises were challenging, exactly what I wanted. During my workouts, other top athletes were also working hard around me. I saw Natalie Coughlin, the Cal swimmer destined for the Olympics. Jerry Rice, the famous wide receiver, was often there too. There were professional athletes recovering from knee surgeries similar in some ways to my own injury. One of them, seeing my ragged scar, asked me jokingly, "Where did you have your knee surgery done? Bosnia?" I left every session in good spirits with my leg fully wrapped in ice, and I fell asleep in the car while Mom drove home. I worked hard and the workout routine helped me achieve my goal of strengthening and regaining the use of my leg.

In addition to exercise, massage was very important for proper healing and rehabilitation, the doctor explained. He said massaging the scars would prevent the scar tissue from becoming tight and inflexible, which could ultimately limit the range of motion in my knee and the muscles of my leg.

Grandma McClellan flew out to California from Wisconsin. She sat with me on the sofa for hours each day, offering comforting words and patiently massaging my leg to help heal the scars. She was happy to make this her task. Her healing touch was important in my long-term recovery and made her feel important too. During our special time together we talked about my goals, she told me stories of her life, and we developed a close bond. This special relationship with my grandmother was an unexpected blessing from the shark and an extension of the closeness I'd already known with my immediate family.

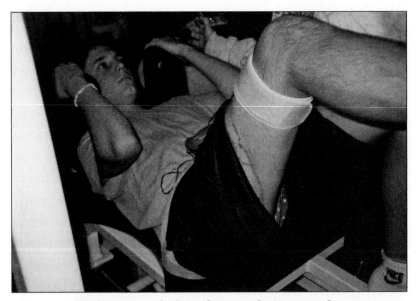

Working on rehab and strengthening my leg

Family, faith, and friendship became increasingly important in our lives.

In the coming weeks, frequent appointments at the hospital, doctors' offices, and physical therapy sessions were overwhelming and time consuming. Walking on crutches was a slow process. Every day I was exhausted just trying to get around.

The orthopedic surgeon scheduled another surgery to remove the screw from my leg. The surgery didn't worry me and I didn't think it would be a big deal after all I'd been through with the shark. But I knew it was difficult for Mom. Sitting in the waiting room reminded her of the surgery on that long night not so long ago. This time the surgery went quickly and smoothly, much easier than a shark attack. I kept the screw on my desk as a reminder of my survival.

Gradually I felt stronger and ready for new challenges. I wanted to get back to schoolwork, friends, and life beyond the shark. But forgetting this life-changing experience wouldn't be easy; I came to realize I would never forget it.

After two months of recovery at home, I returned to school on crutches with a full-length leg brace. Mom drove me to the neighborhood Starbucks each morning where I met up with my friend and classmate, Phil, who gave me rides to school. I sat in the backseat of his car keeping my leg fully outstretched in a solid leg immobilizer.

The day I returned to school, my history teacher played the theme music from *Jaws* when I entered the classroom. We all laughed. I was becoming accustomed to sharks and shark jokes in my life.

It was good to be back at school with friends. The kids surrounded me in the hallways, asking lots of questions.

They wanted to hear all the details because they found the shark story exciting and intriguing. I became more aware of the universal fascination with sharks.

Each evening when I returned home, I tried to catch up on homework and projects I'd missed, but I was always too tired and I just fell asleep. Mom was constantly on the phone with my school counselor trying to intervene, to keep me from losing an entire semester of school.

As soon as I was able, I rejoined the St. Ignatius swim team, participating in practices and swim meets. It took some hard work. And even though I had little chance of winning a heat, the competition and excitement were invigorating and my teammates encouraged me to keep working.

A film crew from *High School Sports Focus*, a Bay Area television program, came to school to cover my story and my ongoing recovery. They filmed as I swam laps in the pool with my team. I hoped that my story and my determination might encourage other young athletes to keep trying too.

For weeks and even months, reporters continued to call while I was recovering at home. TV news crews arrived at our house with their satellite vans, cameras, and lights, and they inevitably showed up right at dinnertime, rushing for a deadline. I was happy to answer their questions and tell my story over and over, but the interviews always took longer than expected. Frequently the reporters became engrossed in the strength of our family and in learning more about sharks. My family and I began to realize how the media shaped lives. I tried to give priority to programs that were educational, sharing valid information about sharks. I refused interviews that were simply looking for sensational value.

A family celebration after the attack

Brothers are best friends

With all the recent news, it seemed that wherever I went in our community, people recognized me. Kids ran up to ask for my autograph. When I signed my name I added a positive message to inspire them, "Never give up . . . always keep trying . . . you can do anything." I began to realize I'd become a sort of role model for these young people and I wanted to help them set goals and overcome challenges in their lives.

Life and schoolwork gradually returned to normal for me and I became stronger, but memories were difficult to erase. Each time I heard a helicopter fly overhead or read about a shark in the news, I was reminded of my blessings. I thought of how close I came that day. One day I was a child, and the next day without warning I saw the thin line between life and death. I fought to live. The shark had made me more aware of the unexpected force of nature and how fragile life could be. I gained a deeper spiritual understanding of my life and my reasons for living. I was aware of how quickly everything could change. The shark was a part of my life I could never forget.

The shark left its mark on my family too. We grew to know how important we were, and are, to each other. We supported each other through a difficult time and we realized how fortunate we were to have each other. We knew life could change in an instant. Together we moved forward as a family, forever touched by the memories.

Every year on August 26, the day of the shark, we celebrate the happy ending to one chapter in our lives. Even now, when I cross the Golden Gate Bridge I look out over the Pacific Ocean toward the Farallon Islands and remember the shark.

LIFE AFTER THE SHARK

"Jonathan taught us to embrace challenge
as an opportunity."
—Eric Kathrein

As a young person growing up in our advanced society, I'd never known what it meant to fear for your life. Death at age sixteen wasn't on my horizon. Wow, the shark changed my world and my perspective on life.

My physical injuries were life threatening. I was incapacitated, unable to walk and lucky to be alive. The doctors watched for infection and I worried this might lead them to amputate my leg. My surgeon said the shark had torn away, or eaten, muscles of my hip that might limit my ability to lift my leg to the side. But after a year of physical therapy, other muscles learned to compensate. I'm now able to run and lift my leg in ways the doctors didn't expect. I may always have some residual pain in my knee, but I can participate fully in activities and sports. I'm proud of my recovery, but it's been an uphill battle.

The emotional scars would take longer to mend. After my experience with the shark I began to fear the ocean and the open water. To me it didn't matter why the shark attacked. Being mistaken for a seal didn't make me feel any better or safer in the water.

At the urging of my brothers I joined them on trips to the beach, but I was afraid to enter the water. I stayed on shore with my camera. The ocean seemed dangerous and hostile. I was too frightened to venture into the water even ankle deep. My brothers understood, and they were patient, but they also wanted to help me overcome the fear.

I didn't want to see Stinson Beach again, but I finally agreed to return for the filming of a "survivor" interview with the *Dateline NBC* crew. The producer wanted actual footage of the beach where the shark attack took place.

I arrived early at Stinson with my family at my side, and Sean met us there too. Seeing the beach again wasn't easy for any of us and the memories came flooding back. My leg brace made walking difficult and I felt unsteady on the beach I knew so well, where I once felt safe. This was not the path I envisioned for my life.

The beach looked like a movie set with lights, reflectors, cameras, director chairs, and electrical cords running across the sand. Eric and Michael ran ahead to check out all the equipment.

Soon the lights and cameras were rolling and the questions began. The interview led to some tough questions.

"Jonathan, how did your shark attack change you?"

"I understand how fragile life can be and how quickly things can change. Some people said I must have had a guardian angel watching over me that day."

Dateline *NBC crew filming at Stinson Beach*

My family and the NBC producer at Stinson Beach

Dateline *NBC interview at the beach*

Warning sign at Stinson Beach

Next he turned to Sean and I listened as Sean told his story. I wanted to know what he remembered. I'd never really heard him talk about that day.

"I had an eerie feeling in the water that day," Sean said. "I wasn't comfortable out there. Something bothered me about the day. Maybe that's why I felt cold and headed to shore."

Sean's words surprised me, but I guess we all have eerie feelings in the water from time to time. He seemed to fear the water now, too.

Finally the reporter asked me one more question. "Jonathan, have you forgiven the shark for what it did to you?"

"What happened to me was not the shark's fault," I said. "The shark was living peacefully in the ocean, doing what it's supposed to do. I was in the shark's world. I've learned that sharks are magnificent and important in our oceans. I'd like to help protect them."

The reporter seemed surprised to hear that I did not express animosity for my attacker. By now I'd learned so much about threats to sharks' survival, I wanted to defend their existence in the delicate ocean environment.

After the interviews, Sean and I walked to the edge of the ocean. Gentle waves washed up onto the sand and I breathed the familiar salt air.

"Do you think you'll ever go back in the water?" Sean asked.

"I guess I don't know yet," I replied. "I definitely want to." I studied the waves, thinking about his question and hoping for my eventual return to the surf. As I looked out across the ocean I discovered something promising I hadn't noticed earlier. I could see the familiar world of the ocean awaiting me, offering new challenges and adventures. I remembered why I loved the ocean.

With Sean at Stinson Beach

Though I would never forget the shark attack, I was ready to move forward.

For my birthday my brothers gave me a shiny new skim board and encouraged me to join them in the water. I could glide on the thin layer of water at the edge of the beach where waves roll out, getting only my feet wet. This was a step forward.

Overcoming the memories wasn't easy but gradually I became more brave or perhaps more determined. I might never fully overcome the fear, but I would not let it dominate my life. There are many dangers on land, too, but we don't stay home because of them.

Years after my attack, I was ready to try surfing again. Michael, Eric, and our friend Charlie, an experienced surfer, teamed up to help me. We loaded our boards and headed out to Cronkite Beach. Breezing along with the windows down and my hair blowing reminded me of so many beach days. Once again we were following along the winding road past familiar scenery and the beach was waiting for us.

I walked tentatively to the edge of the water with Michael, Eric, and Charlie next to me, carrying our surfboards under our arms. Conditions were nearly perfect, with shoulder-high waves breaking in smooth arcs. I stood looking out at the ocean and wondered if I was ready. I just needed a little more time. Eric stood beside me giving me his own quiet support.

"C'mon, let's go, Jonathan," Charlie shouted.

"What are you waiting for?" Michael asked. "You can do it."

"I don't know. Okay, I'm ready."

The three surfers rushed ahead into the water, slid onto their boards, then turned and waited. I lingered in the shallow water, torn between my love for the ocean and my uncertainty. With a deep breath, I tossed my new board across the water and plunged forward into the freedom of the ocean. I remembered the chill and the familiar taste of salt water. Together we paddled out, shoulder to shoulder, into the vast Pacific.

As we got out to the lineup Eric shouted, "Get ready, here comes a good one. This one is yours, Jonathan."

The swell rose. I paddled hard to catch the wave and popped up on my board. Riding the wave required my full concentration and focus. I couldn't think of anything else. I was happy to be back in the ocean.

I remember a reporter once saying, "It's not that I envy what you've had to go through. But, it almost seems to have

Three brothers paddling out

Happy to be back in the water again

made you a richer person." This observation seemed so true. Life had changed for me. Really everything became completely different having faced the ocean's fiercest elements. I'd gained a desire to consume, not material things, but life and life's experiences. I began to spend more time with people and more time outdoors. I wanted to travel more, experience other cultures, and spend time with my friends and family, treating them the best I possibly could.

I started to think about ways I might use my story to help others overcome challenges in their lives. I didn't have a business plan; I just wanted to share my gift with others who might benefit from it. I wanted others to know I didn't hate the shark and, as in all of life, we should not hate our attackers. I wanted to carry my message forward, to do something meaningful with my life.

After graduating from UC Berkeley, searching for a way to help others, I partnered with Richard, my friend Charlie's father, to start a nonprofit organization, Future Leaders For Peace, with a goal to help young people. Our mission was to inspire young people with positive ways to approach life's challenges and dreams. Speaking at student assemblies across Hawaii, California, England, and South Africa, I shared the positive lessons I'd learned from the shark with hundreds of young people. As I looked out at the faces of the students at the conclusion of each of my speeches, I could see understanding in their eyes and joy in their smiles. I knew I'd made an impact in their young lives.

I wrote a children's book, *Don't Fear the Shark*, using the shark attack as a metaphor for our lives. I wanted to inspire young people to nurture their relationships and

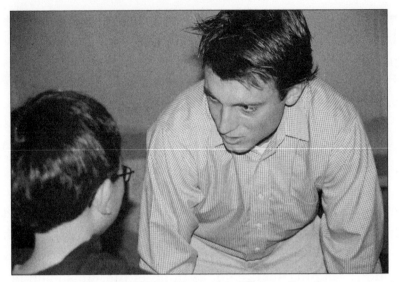

Motivational speaking with "Future Leaders
for Peace" to help children

to respect the world around them. The message of the book is that we must treat others better, and not hate our attackers.

As a speaking coach and consultant, I've traveled the world leading seminars and teaching public speaking to executives. Research shows that most people fear public speaking more than anything else, even more than death or shark attacks. I enjoy helping others, offering them new techniques and skills, inspiring them to succeed. I'm happy I can help others gain confidence to overcome their fear.

Now, as a father, I'm teaching my little daughter to love and respect the ocean as much as I do. I share my joy with her at the beach, teaching her about the ocean and its magnificent creatures. I envision the day when she will join me in the waves. She squeals with excitement and

The face of the future—my little daughter,
Madison, with me at the beach

Three brothers surfing together on a family trip to Hawaii

Surfing with my family on a trip to the Dominican Republic

waves to me as I paddle out on my surfboard, letting me know she's ready to explore the world with me, reminding me of all I've gained. When I look back to shore from the water, I can see her smiling face, the face of the future.

LEARNING ABOUT SHARKS

"Sharks don't mean to eat people . . .
Maybe the shark thought I was trying to hurt it . . .
Maybe it was afraid of me . . .
Maybe it was all just a big mistake."
—Jonathan Kathrein

My first oceanography lesson came with a phone call from a world-renowned shark expert while I was lying flat on my back in the hospital bed. He sparked my interest with his wealth of information about sharks, especially the one I had encountered. I began to appreciate sharks as highly skilled hunters with extremely acute senses. I was eager to learn more. My fascination led me from nearly being killed by a shark to becoming a spokesperson to help protect sharks.

I wanted to learn more about the great white shark's behavior, where it lives, and why it attacks. Over the next few days and months of my recovery, while trying to forget the pain, I talked to many shark experts. My observations also helped researchers who were interested in knowing what I saw and felt.

I learned that more great white sharks live in the Red Triangle than anywhere else in the world. Anyone who enters the waters of the Pacific, especially in the Red Triangle, is swimming in the presence of sharks. I also learned that generally the sharks never bother people.

Experts explained that a person on a board makes a perfect target for the great white shark because the silhouette resembles a seal from below. A surfer in a wetsuit on the surface of the water looks like a seal, the shark's favorite food. I was learning about the ocean in a very real and meaningful way.

Scientists have described the white shark as a mugger. A trickster. It attacks from below and behind, and its victim does not see it coming. This technique matched my own experience. The shark bumped me without creating a ripple and swam past me with its dark coloring making it invisible. It returned like a mugger, attacking me suddenly from beneath and behind.

I learned that the search for food motivates the shark's instincts. However, the white shark is a picky predator that prefers seals and sea lions to humans. But people can be in danger if they are in the shark's territory, especially if they look like food. The great white is the largest flesh-eating shark on the planet and the most dangerous shark to humans in temperate waters.

After I came home from the hospital, Dr. John McCosker invited my family and me to visit him and tour the laboratory of the Steinhardt Aquarium at the California Academy of Sciences in San Francisco. We eagerly accepted his offer on a Saturday afternoon. It was a chance for us to learn more about the white shark that had impacted our lives.

Dr. McCosker gave us a personal behind-the-scenes tour of his laboratory, the archives, and the collections of the aquarium. The basement laboratory was mysterious and fascinating to my brothers and to me. Tall floor-to-ceiling shelves lined with glass jars that held specimens of rare and sometimes weird sea creatures. We saw bottles containing samples of unusual fish collected by researchers on trips into the deep Pacific. He showed us various types of smaller sharks preserved in tanks, with a close-up look at their jaws and teeth. He pulled his favorite samples off the shelves and told stories of his studies and trips to great depths of the sea.

My family and I were intrigued by his wealth of information and appreciative of his generosity in sharing his knowledge. He knew more about sharks than anyone else

My family with Dr. McCosker touring the laboratory at the Steinhart Aquarium, California Academy of Sciences

in the world. A friendship developed between us based on our mutual interest and experiences. We quickly realized that Dr. McCosker was not only the most knowledgeable and respected shark expert in the world, he was extremely cordial and entertaining as well.

Shark scientists recognize the Farallon Islands as a major habitat for great white sharks. The islands are close enough to be seen from the Golden Gate Bridge, yet not well-known even by locals because of their remote and hostile setting. This inhospitable yet complex and fragile environment supports an abundance of marine life and provides a smorgasbord of food for great white sharks. Seals and sea lions crowd onto rocky ledges to sun themselves, while sharks circle and wait for an opportunity for a surprise attack.

The jagged peaks of the islands emerge on the horizon like an otherworldly silhouette rising from the depths of turbulent cobalt water. I'd seen them many times while crossing the Golden Gate Bridge on my way to school in San Francisco. The islands are only twenty-seven miles west of San Francisco and twenty-six miles from Stinson Beach, but getting there by boat can be a turbulent ride through rough, choppy waters. Visitors are not allowed to step onto the islands, which are part of a protected marine sanctuary inhabited by seals, birds, and sharks living together in a balance that is as fragile as it is obscure. For millions of years, the islands have existed as a world unto themselves, shrouded in fog and mystery. The islands are just five miles from the edge of the continental shelf where the ocean floor plunges two miles into darkness.

Surfers might be tempted by the waves breaking along the islands. But no one would be so foolish as to take a chance of becoming live bait out there. The islands are notoriously rugged, remote, treacherous, and surrounded by sharks.

A calm day on a boat at the Farallon Islands, the tip of the Red Triangle

The islands are the heart of the Gulf of the Farallones National Marine Sanctuary that spans 1,279 square miles of coastal water north and west of San Francisco. Here cold nutrient-rich water from the deep ocean flows into the more shallow sunlit waters of the sanctuary, supporting a tapestry of life. The sanctuary is a globally significant ecosystem with thousands of birds, blue, grey, and humpback whales, elephant and harbor seals, threatened Steller sea lions, as well as one of the largest white shark populations anywhere on the planet. The islands are a global white shark hotspot.

133

Four species of pinnipeds live and breed on the islands: California sea lions, Steller sea lions, harbor seals, and northern elephant seals. They offer a plentiful buffet of the white shark's favorite food. As a result of the abundance of seals, the islands and the surrounding waters have become the home and feeding grounds for great white sharks. This complex environment, with its cold water, abundance of marine life, and rich upwelling current has given the adjacent coastline of Marin County, including Stinson Beach, the nickname "White Shark Central."

Numbers relating to shark attacks are not easy to verify, and sometimes they are based only on hearsay rather than on reliable evidence. Worldwide statistics are difficult to compile because shark attacks frequently happen in remote places and sometimes they are not reported at all. We confirmed numbers of white shark attacks along the California coast with the help of Dr. John McCosker, Senior Scientist and Chair of the Department of Aquatic Biology at the California Academy of Sciences in San Francisco. Dr. McCosker is a renowned shark expert who has published numerous books and scientific journal articles, and he is a leading expert who travels the world speaking and researching sharks. John McCosker and Robert Lea publish a scientific review of white shark attacks every ten years.

In California, from 1950 to 2011, there were 105 verifiable unprovoked white shark attacks. Of these 105 attacks, only thirteen or fourteen of them were fatalities. In one instance, two kayakers left from Paradise Cove, Malibu, and did not return. The woman's body, showing evidence of shark attack, was found, but the man's was not. It might be presumed he died from an attack but there is no evidence

134

to support this. The most recent shark attack fatality in California occurred in 2010 with the death of a nineteen-year-old boogie boarder off Vandenberg Air Force Base in Santa Barbara County, California. The Wall Street Journal reports that in 2011 fatal shark attacks reached their highest level in two decades, but there were no fatal attacks in the US in 2011.

California has had 105 shark attacks in the past sixty-one years, an average of one or two attacks per year, with one to four attacks in any single recent year. Compared to deaths from automobile accidents, shark attacks are a lower risk. The likelihood of shark attacks is relatively lower than the other perils we face in life. However, exact comparisons are impossible because people spend an unknown number of hours in the water versus pursuing other activities. In any event, an attack by a great white shark is never an insignificant encounter, especially to the victim and the family of the victim.

Most attempts to hold great white sharks in captivity for any extended length of time have failed. These sharks simply do not thrive for very long in captivity. One problem is that great white sharks are big; they can grow up to twenty-one feet long and weigh as much as 7,000 pounds. An animal that large needs a lot of space, making it hard to hold it in any kind of tank. In addition, electromagnetic fields in steel and concrete tanks confuse the shark's delicate navigation senses. Great whites can pick up electrical charges as small as 0.005 microvolt, the amount of energy generated by a beating heart or a gill action. The Steinhart Aquarium tried to keep a healthy seven-and-a-half-foot white shark named "Sandy" that was brought to the

The great white shark, taken at Guadalupe Island, Mexico

Photos courtesy of David McGuire

aquarium in 1980, but the shark kept bumping the metal seams in the tank and, as a result, was released back into the wild.

In August 2011 the Monterey Bay Aquarium held a four-foot eight-inch young great white shark for fifty-five days. I had the opportunity to see this small great white shark swimming with other fish in a large tank at the aquarium. Seeing this young shark was exciting because it was one of the few great whites to feed and survive even briefly in captivity.

To me, this small great white shark looked like a Ferrari in a tank full of Volkswagens. It was beautiful and sleek, highly evolved. Even its relatively small presence caused the other larger fish to be on guard. When it was dropped into the tank, even the imposing six-foot five hundred pound tuna, which normally ruled the tank, began to school at the far end. In every situation, the preeminence of the great white shark is without question. I will always respect this majestic creature that once held me but let me go.

Ultimately, the decision to release the shark after fifty-five days was based on changes in how well it was navigating the exhibit and concern that the shark was not thriving in captivity. Five other great white sharks have been returned to the wild after spending from eleven days to six months in the aquarium. With few opportunities to see white sharks, the public's impression of the great white depends mostly on photographs and descriptions by those who have seen one, or as it has been wrongfully portrayed in popular media.

The great white shark, taken at Guadalupe Island, Mexico
Photos courtesy of David McGuire

The shark is the object of great fascination to many. The power of the great white shark stirs a primeval curiosity in young and old. People I meet are fascinated by my experience with the shark because the great white shark is legendary, and yet so rarely observed.

After my attack, a reporter from *Surfer* magazine called to interview me when a shark was sighted off the coast. Sharks are always out there, I reminded the reporter, and sometimes people spot them. Whenever there's a shark attack, it's serious for the victim, but unfortunately it often becomes a news story reinforcing the undeserved vicious stereotype of sharks.

White shark populations and attacks on humans in California have increased in recent years, along with the increase in the seal population due to laws protecting seals. And yet, even with greater recreational use of California's coastal waters, there have been surprisingly few attacks on humans. Of the millions of people who enter the ocean each year, most are never touched and most never see a shark in their lifetime. In reality, our fears of sharks are much greater than the actual risk associated with the world's most fascinating creature.

SHARK SCIENCE

"Sharks are essential members of a healthy
ocean ecosystem."
—David McGuire, Director and Founder of Sea Stewards

When people hear the word "shark" they think of the powerful shape and familiar jaws of the great white shark. The pronounced dorsal fin, the torpedo-shaped body, and the great white grin are unmistakable. From Bruce, the mechanical shark of *Jaws* ruthlessly sawing Quint in half, to the toothy grin of the cartoon shark in *Finding Nemo*, the image of teeth and blood and the great white killing machine are equated with the word "shark."

Our perceptions of sharks and shark behavior are driven more by media and movies than real life. What is a shark? Sharks come from an ancient lineage of fish adapting to every shape and size. Sharks are amazingly diverse, filling nearly every ecological niche in the oceans from mud sucker to apex predator. Shark species vary in length from the pygmy shark, a few inches in length, to the mighty whale shark, measuring up to forty-five feet. Of the approximately 450 different species, almost half are less than a meter long. Although a white shark's teeth can slice through muscle and bone, some shark's teeth can't shred paper. So what makes a shark a shark?

Sharks are fish that belong to the class Chondrichthyes, a diverse group of rays, skates, and true sharks. The latter consist of the Squalidae, like the spiny dogfish and leopard sharks of the San Francisco Bay, and the lamnid sharks, like the mako and white sharks. A weird sister group called the Chimaera, also known as ratfish or ghostfish, live in the deeper waters offshore and look nothing like what we think of as a shark.

The common characteristic that separates the sharks, skates, and rays and chimaera from bony fish like tuna and swordfish is a skeleton made completely of cartilage: the same tissue that is in our ear lobes, nose, and joints. Cartilage is like the carbon fiber of nature. It gives the support of bone, but is much lighter than bone. This structural material keeps sharks lighter so they don't sink, and allows sharks to be extremely flexible. These unique advantages have allowed them to survive for millions of years. This cartilage may also be the undoing of many shark species.

Sharks predate bony fish by millions of years and they have filled nearly every place in the food web from apex predator to detritivore ("trash eater" to the layman). Sharks range from the biggest fish in the sea—whale sharks—to flat sharks like thornback rays with teeth like flat plates.

Sharks, extremely successful in the ocean, have survived several major extinction events, including the one that killed the dinosaurs sixty-five million years ago. Along the way they have developed an extraordinary toolkit of senses to help them survive. Sharks have many adaptations, particular abilities and characteristics, that allow them to survive in their environment. However, the survival of the great white shark is now in question as it faces the biggest threat of all—man.

Sense of smell: Among the adaptations that have allowed sharks to survive successfully, sharks have developed sophisticated sensory organs to detect prey. If you look at a shark head-on, the first thing you notice (if you can ignore the teeth and the urge to swim away) is the very prominent snout. Some people have likened sharks to giant swimming noses. Sharks smell using nostrils in the lower forepart of the nose. Testing by researchers confirms that sharks have an exceptional sense of smell.

As the shark swims, water flows through two forward-facing nostrils positioned along the sides of the snout. Sharks swim in a sinuous motion moving their head to scan the water. Water enters the nasal passage and moves past folds of skin covered with sensory cells. In some species of sharks, these sensitive cells can detect even the slightest traces of blood in the water. Most sharks can detect blood and animal odors from many miles away. This sensitivity is so acute that a great white shark would be able to detect a single drop of blood in an Olympic pool.

A shark's sense of smell is also directional, allowing it to hone in on a scent trail. The twin nasal cavities act something like our ears. Just as we can distinguish when directional sounds are louder on one side than the other, the shark's nose can detect when smells are more intense on one side than the other. In this way, a shark can determine the direction the smell is coming from and swim in that direction.

143

Breathing: Like bony fish, sharks breathe by extracting dissolved oxygen from water. Water enters the mouth, passes through the gills, and is expelled through gill slits behind the head. These slits are covered in the bony fish, but the gills on elasmobranchs (Latin for "armored gill") are prominent alongside the head. As the water flows through the gill openings, it passes a series of tiny gill filaments. These filaments are covered with microscopic blood-filled capillaries that have lower oxygen content than the water around them. This imbalance causes oxygen in the water to diffuse into the shark's bloodstream, where it is distributed throughout the body.

Some sharks, like the bottom dwelling leopard and smooth-hound sharks in San Francisco Bay, have a gill pump. A set of muscles sucks in water and pushes it past the gills. Like our lungs, which extract oxygen into our bloodstream while we are at rest, these sharks can continuously gather oxygen while sedentary.

Larger sharks extract oxygen from the water using a different method called ram ventilation. Water passes over the gills as the shark swims. Active sharks like the blue and white sharks depend on ram ventilation almost entirely, which means they stay in motion most of the time. This adaptation can also be a shark's undoing. If caught on a longline set for tuna, the shark cannot swim and will suffocate and die.

An additional type of organ shared by many sharks is spiracles, small pores located behind the eye of several more sedentary species. This organ is lost in the big fast-swimming sharks but common to slower-moving sharks like local Bay Area spiny dogfish and rays and skates that live along the bottom. These additional openings allow the fish to pump oxygenated water directly to a special blood vessel leading to the brain and eyes. The larger, more developed spiracle in rays and skates provides flow to the respiratory system, allowing the flat sharks to breathe while their gills are submerged in the sediments.

Electromagnetic Sensors: One of the amazing adaptations unique to sharks is the ability to detect electromagnetic fields as well as temperature gradients through an organ called the ampullae of Lorenzini. Ampullae are small pores consisting of a network of clusters of electrically sensitive receptor cells positioned under the skin in the shark's head. Most of the ampullae are clustered symmetrically around the nose and head. The ampullae pores are plainly visible as dark spots in the skin.

Specialized cells are connected to pores on the skin's surface via small gel-filled vessels or ampullae. Each ampulla consists of a jelly-filled canal bundle of sensory cells containing multiple nerve fibers. These fibers are enclosed in a gel-filled tubule that has a direct opening to the surface through a pore. The gel is a glycoprotein-based substance with the same electrical resistivity as seawater and has electrical properties similar to a semiconductor. They provide the ability to detect electromagnetic fields as well as temperature gradients.

These sensors let the shark receive weak electrical fields generated by living organisms. Every time an animal moves it generates an electrical field, and even heartbeats emit a faint electrical pulse. If it's close enough, the shark can detect even the faint electrical field generated by a low voltage battery. Great whites are so sensitive they can detect half a billionth of a volt.

Hearing: Sharks also have an acute sense of hearing. Research suggests they can hear low frequency sounds far below our range of hearing. Sharks hear best at frequencies below 1,000 Hertz, which is the range of most natural sounds in the marine environment. This sense of hearing helps sharks locate potential prey swimming and splashing in the water. Sharks may track sounds over many miles, listening for distress sounds from wounded prey. Although untested, it is also highly probable that sharks can detect and follow underwater vocalizations by pinnipeds and cetaceans.

Vision: Although it was once thought that sharks had very poor vision, we now know that sharks have sharp vision. Research shows that a shark's eyes may be more than ten times as sensitive to light as humans' eyes, giving them better underwater vision. Scientists also believe that sharks may be farsighted, able to see better at distance rather than closeup, due to the structure of the eye. Vision varies among species of sharks due to differences in the size, focusing ability, and strength of the eyes.

Eyesight varies from species to species of sharks. Some less active sharks stay near the water's surface and have less acute vision than those living in deep water like the six and seven-gilled sharks. Sharks have an ability to open and close the pupil in response to differing light situations, similar to humans. Like humans, a shark's eye includes a cornea, iris, lens, and retina. Rods and cones located in the shark's retina allow the shark to see in differing light situations as well as to see color and detail. In addition, sharks, similar to cats, have a mirror-like layer in the back of the eye referred to as the tapetum lucidum.

This layer further increases the intensity of incoming light, enhancing the eye's sensitivity to light. The tapetum lucidum makes sharks particularly adept at seeing under water. This tissue consists of mirrored crystals, allowing the shark to contract and dilate its pupil in much the same way we do. When light enters the eye, it is reflected back to the retina instead of being absorbed, which allows the shark better visibility in the darkness of the deep ocean. Sharks that are more active at night (nocturnal) have better developed tapetum lucidum tissue.

Sharks don't have eyelids but protect their eyes with a special layer called a nictitating membrane. This is a protective mechanism used during hunting when prey or other sharks are struggling and biting around the head and delicate eye area. This membrane, similar to that of dogs and cats, acts as a shield during attacks. The visible but transparent membrane slides from under the eyelid to cover the entire eyeball. White sharks can also roll their eyes back in their heads. When a white shark attacks, it rolls its eyes back, making them appear white, and temporarily blinding the shark. In these final moments of an attack, the shark must rely on its other senses to finish off the prey.

White sharks have been known to spy-hop, raising their heads above the surface like whales to visually reconnoiter. Given their light sensitivity it is unknown how well sharks see above water, but researchers and observers have reported sharks rising up and giving them a good long look.

Touch or Feel: Another unique sense organ is the shark's lateral line, an adaption shared by bony fish. The lateral line is a channel running along the flanks beneath the shark's skin. The two channels run on both sides of the body from the shark's head all the way to its tail. Water flowing across the surface of the shark enters the channels through pores on the skin's surface. The insides of the main tubes are lined with hair-like protrusions called neuromasts that act like the sensory organs in our inner ear, which are connected to sensory nerves. Physical impulses caused by prey swimming nearby stimulate the sensory organ, alerting the shark to any potential prey or predators in the area.

Jaws: An amazing ability, and one that creates a memorable image, is the ability of the large sharks to project their lower jaw away and out from the skull. In most vertebrates the lower jaw moves freely but the upper jaw is firmly attached to the skull. In sharks, the upper jaw rests below the skull and can be detached when the shark attacks its prey. White shark jaws are separated from the lower skull. When attacking large prey like elephant seals, the shark unhinges its jaw allowing the shark to debilitate the seal with its formidable rows of teeth.

The shark's great investigatory organ and its best weapon is its mouth. Sharks often investigate prey with a test bite and then release them. This is thought to be the cause of many attacks on humans. Many shark species rely on their sense of taste and test their meal before consumption. Taste buds clustered in the mouth analyze the potential meal to see if it's palatable. Sharks often reject prey after the first bite if it is outside their ordinary diet. This could explain why so many shark attack victims survive white shark attacks.

The taste as well as texture of a human, a wetsuit, or a surfboard may be enough for a shark to realize this is not a favored prey, and to continue its hunt. Studies of attacks on inanimate objects suggest that attacks on people are not for the purpose of consumption but only for the purpose of investigation. Frequently, teeth marks and even teeth are left behind, allowing forensic scientists to match the species with the attack.

Teeth: Shark teeth are as diverse as sharks, highly specialized and variable among the different species. Some bottom-dwelling sharks, like the common leopard sharks, have special grinding teeth for cracking shells, and basking sharks that swim in the Gulf of the Farallones outside the Golden Gate don't have teeth, but a series of baleen-like plates that filter plankton.

Sharks that go after larger prey like elephant seals have a different feeding strategy and require different teeth. White sharks tear their prey, sawing and biting off large pieces of flesh. Many sharks, like the sevengill shark, have combinations of long, pointed teeth and wider, serrated teeth so they can hold their prey in place while they cut into it. The local Bay Area seven-gilled shark has sharp, jagged upper teeth that grasp, and comb-shaped lower teeth that saw the flesh of prey. The cookie cutter shark literally sucks on its prey with the upper lip and teeth while the lower teeth act as a circular saw, using its body to rotate a plug out of unsuspecting whales, fish, and sometimes even people, as experienced by a distance swimmer in Hawaii.

Shark teeth consist of hard enamel like our teeth, but they don't rest in the jaw like most vertebrates' teeth. Shark teeth are attached to the jaw by soft tissue. New sharper teeth continually replace worn or broken teeth in a kind of conveyor mechanism. Sharks can lose thousands of teeth in a lifetime.

Great white sharks have about 3,000 teeth, arranged in several rows. The teeth are triangularly shaped with serrations on the edges and can measure up to three inches long. The first two rows of teeth are used for grabbing and cutting their prey. Teeth in the last rows rotate into place when the front teeth are broken, worn, or fall out.

Tails and fins: Sharks differ from most bony fish in the way they move through the water. Once a white shark has sensed the presence of prey, it uses its incredibly strong tail to propel it through the water. Sharks deftly maneuver through the water by adjusting the angle of their fins for lift and depression.

Sharks have two sets of paired pectoral fins on the sides of their body that are used like the wings of an airplane. The shark can position these fins at different angles, changing the pressure of the water moving around them. Like a wing, when the shark tilts a fin up, the water flows across it so there is greater pressure below the fin than above, creating lift. When the shark tilts the fin down, the greater pressure above the fin pushes the shark down.

Sharks have one or two vertical dorsal fins and a vertical anal fin on the ventral (underside) surface. These fins act like the vertical stabilizers of a plane, with the tail fin acting as the propeller.

Another distinction from bony fish is that sharks don't have a swim bladder. The shark's buoyancy is regulated by the high oil content in its liver. This oil, high in vitamin A, was one of the reasons San Francisco Bay Area sharks, especially soupfin and seven-gilled sharks, were heavily fished during World War II. Before Vitamin A became chemically synthesized, the local shark populations were nearly fished out for their oil. They were fished again in tournaments in the Bay Area in the '70s and early '80s after the movie *Jaws*. Scientists believe the local San Francisco Bay population may have just recently recovered from that fishing effort.

Body Temperature: A fantastic adaptation among some of the large lamnid sharks, like mako sharks and white sharks, is body temperature regulation. Most fish are considered ectotherms with body temperatures closely matching that of the external environment. Because of a special adaptation called the "rete mirabile" (Latin for "wonderful net"), lamnid sharks have a body temperature exceeding the external water temperature. This web-like structure of veins and arteries, located along each lateral side of the shark, conserves heat by warming the cooler arterial blood with the venous blood that has been warmed by the working muscles. This maintains certain parts of the body (particularly the stomach and brain) at temperatures up to twenty-five degrees Fahrenheit above that of the surrounding water, while the heart and gills remain at sea temperature.

The core body temperature of the shark can also drop to match its surroundings to conserve energy. This allows these sharks to hunt in colder waters in areas like the Pacific coast near San Francisco. Cold water and high activity levels place high metabolic demands on the shark, requiring high-caloric food such as the fats stored in elephant seals.

Shark Skin: Sharks have unusual skin, without the larger, more prominent scales found in bony fish. Rather, sharks have a skin composed of placoid scales. Sharks are covered with these smaller scales, called denticles, that resemble small teeth. These tough protective denticles are aligned so they channel water over the shark's body, minimizing drag due to friction. The tough skin of the shark has been used by native peoples as a form of leather, and the rough surface is also useful as sandpaper. Modern applications similar to shark's skin include the synthetic specialized coatings on boat hulls that have lower resistance to the water than a smooth surface.

Reproduction: Most fish, like rockfish, have millions or even billions of eggs in their lifetime. Broadcasting these eggs to the currents of fate, these fish can have huge success rates producing thousands of offspring in good years. Sharks have a different strategy. The reproductive pattern of sharks is more like mammals.

Sharks invest more time and energy into their offspring, and therefore have far fewer young than most fish. Some sharks, like swell sharks, lay eggs in a hard keratin case. Keratin is a fibrous protein such as that contained in hair, feathers, hoofs, and horns. These egg cases attach themselves to kelp or entangle in rocks as the baby shark develops and hatches. Other sharks like white sharks are ovoviviparous, which means that their eggs develop and hatch in the uterus and continue to develop in the body of the parent until birth. Other sharks are viviparous, which means they carry pups in the uterus until giving live birth. The larger sharks have only a few pups, some as few as one each reproductive cycle, which can take two years. Many sharks, like the white sharks, can take a decade to be able to reproduce, and some, like the spiny dogfish, take as many as thirty-five years before they can reproduce.

The birthing process varies from species to species. Some sharks lay eggs in protected areas on the ocean floor or, as with the swell shark, the egg case becomes entangled in the kelp. When the shark pup is fully developed, it breaks through the tough egg case and heads out on its own. Often empty egg cases, known as mermaid's purses, wash ashore.

In most shark species the pups develop inside the womb and are fully formed at birth. Some sharks, such as white sharks and salmon sharks, even feed on their siblings in the womb, a practice called embryophagy. When the shark pups are born they are fully formed, resembling small adult sharks, fully capable of swimming and feeding.

White sharks: Other than feeding, little is known about the white shark's behavior, such as mating and birthing. Great white sharks are ovoviviparous, so their eggs develop and hatch in the uterus and continue to develop in the body of the parent until birth. The exact gestation period is not known for white sharks, but scientists believe it is around a year. Observations at the Farallones indicate some female sharks disappear for two years and then return, leading to speculation that the sharks give birth away from the main population before returning to the aggregation sites. Delivery is in spring and summer.

The white shark litter size ranges from two to ten young (and possibly up to seventeen) pups, each around three-to-four-and-a-half-feet in length at birth. Females mature at twelve to fifteen feet at about fourteen to sixteen years old. Male great whites are slightly smaller and mature at nine to ten years of age. It is believed that the life span of a white shark exceeds thirty years.

Along the west coast of North America, great whites give birth to their young in the warmer waters off Southern California. The juveniles linger in Southern California and then slowly migrate north as they grow larger. According to a recent study by Stanford researchers for the Tagging of Pacific Pelagics (TOPP) and Monterey Bay Aquarium scientists, the white sharks of the Farallones, Tomales Bay, and Año Nuevo migrate to an area between Baja and Hawaii known as "White Shark Café." These sharks join another sub-population of sharks that gather at Guadalupe Island off the coast of Northern Baja and spend at least 100 days there before returning. On the journey out, they swim slowly and dive down to around 3,000 feet. After they arrive, they change behavior and make shorter dives to about 1,000 feet for up to ten minutes. Preliminary genetic studies suggest that the Guadalupe population does not mix with the California population. However, one shark tagged at Guadalupe was tracked north to Año Nuevo. When the sharks return they demonstrate unusual site fidelity, returning to their respective feeding grounds.

Other areas of concentrated white shark populations are found off the coasts of West Australia, New Zealand, and South Africa. In 2009 a white shark tagged off the coast of South Africa swam to the southern coast of Australia and back within the year, a roundtrip of over 7,000 miles. Why white sharks migrate so far and what they do at their destination is not well-known, although the diving profiles suggest they are feeding and possibly mating in this region.

Need for protection: The late onset of reproductive age, long gestation period, rare mating, and the small number of shark pups makes populations of white sharks extremely

Great white shark, taken at Guadalupe Island, Mexico.
Photo courtesy of David McGuire

vulnerable to overfishing. Sharks are frequently caught as by-catch in the Pacific tuna and swordfish longline industry.

When white sharks leave California waters, where they are protected, their vulnerability increases. White sharks cross thousands of miles where longlines are set for swordfish and tuna and where they are vulnerable to being killed as accidental by-catch or caught intentionally for the shark fin trade. One set of shark fins brought $40,000 on the Hong Kong market. As a result of human interactions, the population of white sharks is at risk.

The shark's abilities and adaptations, changes developed over thousands of centuries, make sharks the consummate predator in the sea. With their acute sense of hearing, temperature, vibration, electrical impulses, and smell, sharks are able to sense their prey from long distances. Even in conditions of poor visibility, their superior use of sight, taste, and pressure sensitivity allow the shark to maneuver close to their intended prey. Powerful and specialized jaws make sharks efficient at securing their prey.

With all of their successful adaptations and superior hunting abilities, one would expect white sharks to kill more people than they do, especially considering that most humans are slow, awkward, and flail in the water. How is it that sharks don't attack and eat more humans? Sharks hunting people is more myth than reality. In fact, humans are a greater danger to sharks than sharks are to people.

SHARK BEHAVIOR AND SHARK-HUMAN INTERACTIONS

"One thing we know for sure . . .
the shark is still out there."
—Michael Kathrein

The glistening ebony shape streaks through the waters of the Pacific, moving slightly from side to side as its giant tail powers it through the water without a ripple. Its back is the color of slate from its wide snout to the crescent moon of its tail. The great white shark is mysterious and imposing with its black eyes and sweeping tail. Its smooth body glides with graceful supremacy, flexing as it turns. Smaller fish scatter as it passes.

The shark is as beautiful as it is dangerous as it flexes its powerful muscles, moving through the water with effortless motion. Millions of years of evolution have created a masterpiece of aquatic engineering and sensory capability.

Sharks are among the oldest animals on earth, with the earliest known sharks dating from over 400 million years ago. They are the ocean's dominant large predators, perfectly designed to hunt, eat, and swim. Great white sharks feed on very large prey. They are apex predators, at the top the food chain in the ocean.

The scientific name for the white shark is *Carcharodon carcharias*, commonly known as the "great white shark." It is the largest predatory shark in the sea. Great whites can top out over two tons in weight and over twenty feet in length. Even a twelve-foot shark can weigh thousands of pounds. The great white shark is one of the largest and most deadly predators in the world.

Despite years of study, the great white shark remains shrouded in mystery. Scientists know surprisingly little about its habits and numbers. These sharks are never successfully held in captivity for long and are rarely ever seen in the wild, with relatively few encounters between great white sharks and people. White sharks are the most elusive and mysterious predators on earth, so massive they're like an oceanic dinosaur, so rarely seen they're almost a myth.

The shark prowls unseen in deep dark water beyond the coast, solitary and silent, accompanied only by a small cordon of zebra-striped pilot fish drafting energy and speed from the shark's momentum. The small fish mirror every movement of the shark as its huge muscular body flexes and moves in the near-absence of light. The shark isn't bothered by their presence just inches away. The little fish look miniscule next to their huge companion.

The great creature moves swiftly above the ocean floor. With its sweeping vertical tail, its solid muscular body flexes constantly in a silvery web of flickering light. Its enormous broad back, dark bluish-grey, almost black in hue, is crowned majestically with a dorsal fin.

The great white shark is an aggressive apex predator, an efficient and specialized hunter that can attack large prey because of the power and size of its enormous jaws. It is the top predator of the waters of California's North Coast, the most dangerous coastline in the world. More great white sharks live here than any other place in the world. Although they have been known to attack people, generally they do not eat humans. Unfortunately, sometimes the violent first hit proves fatal.

The first recorded white shark attack on a human on the Northern California coast was on December 7, 1952. A seventeen-year-old boy was swimming with his friends in Monterey Bay when a fifteen-foot great white shark attacked him. He died in the water before he could be brought to shore.

Scientists say the great white shark is the only shark that is a danger to humans on the coast of California. Unprovoked shark attacks on humans are uncommon relative to the numbers of people in the water. However, great white sharks are so prevalent in the waters off the North Coast of California that anyone who enters the ocean here must acknowledge the presence of sharks and the risk of an attack. Shark attacks are a rare occurrence, but extremely serious when they happen.

Surfers were riding the waves on Thanksgiving morning, 2002 at Salmon Creek Beach, a popular surf beach in northern California at the northern tip of the Red Triangle. Suddenly, without warning a huge shark struck a boogie boarder with massive force from below. Rising up through ten feet of water, the shark hit hard and grabbed his legs with its razor-sharp teeth.

Frightened surfers began yelling when they suddenly saw the dorsal fin of a sixteen-foot shark and blood filling the water as the shark tossed their friend into the air. The shark released him just as suddenly as it attacked. His friends helped him to shore where a helicopter arrived and he was airlifted to a nearby hospital for immediate surgery to repair serious injuries.

The teeth marks in his wetsuit were from a great white shark, and the same teeth had left bone-deep lacerations in his leg. Doctors said he was lucky to be alive, especially riding a boogie board. These smaller boards offer less protection than a surfboard and the rider's legs are more exposed. As in most cases, the victim never saw the shark coming.

"It's interesting how rare these attacks are, considering the billions of hours spent in the water by people who are boogie boarding, swimming, and surfing," said shark expert John McCosker.

Great white sharks do not search out humans. Rather, they mistake humans for their normal food, seals and sea lions that live in rocky coastal areas along the Pacific, often the same areas where people surf. Many rocky areas border the surfing and swimming beaches of California. White sharks are most abundant near seal and sea lion colonies because they depend on the fat of the seals and sea lions to survive. One of the best ways to avoid a shark attack is to avoid swimming near concentrations of seals and sea lions, the prey of the great white shark.

The Marine Mammal Protection Act of 1972 protects seals and sea lions, the great white shark's favorite food, in California waters. As a result, the National Oceanic and Atmospheric Administration (NOAA) reports that California sea lion and Pacific harbor seal populations have increased dramatically in recent years, creating an abundant food supply for great white sharks. The increase in seal populations attracts more sharks to the coast, to local beaches, and closer to humans.

On a slate grey morning in 1999, a young woman hiked the narrow trail to a rocky point of Trinidad Head overlooking the Pacific Ocean. The path was a thin line in the ferns, worn by the bare feet of many surfers. She looked out over the waves that scattered into foam on the rocks with the tide going out. The day felt warm even at the coast. The conditions were pristine, the water glassy, and the air calm with almost no wind. The waves were small and inconsistent but still the surf looked good. Out at the horizon she saw the faint rise of a swell that moved toward shore and crashed on the rocks at the far end of the point where a seal swam.

She watched as two other surfers lined up beyond the point, ready to go. With the next breaking wave the surfers did a couple of quick turns down the face of the wave and managed to kick out before hitting the rocks. In spite of the rocks and low tide, she suited up and maneuvered down the trail, feeling a bit shaky about the rocks and the cold water and about surfing without a buddy. She had heard the rumors about shark season, but she had never seen a shark and didn't want to dwell on thoughts of sharks.

She knew the water would be cold, but she plunged ahead and fought the current to get out past the waves beyond the point. With the challenge of tough conditions she didn't want to get caught inside and churned against the rocks so she waited and watched, trying to gauge the best spot to drop into the next wave. Two surfers in black wetsuits rode down the face of the wave just as she realized she was too late to catch this one. She watched for them to turn and swim back out to where she floated on her board.

Suddenly, a huge shadow moved through the water with lightning-fast speed and struck one of the black objects from below. A blur passed before her as a large dorsal fin shot across the surface of the water for about ten feet before the wave passed over and erased it from view. The hit was sudden and exact. The wave obscured her sight, but after it crashed, she saw only one surfer pop up. She knew that a great white shark had attacked and one of the surfers was missing.

She had to get out of there. She lined up fast and took a late drop but the wave was pushing her toward the rocks. She kicked out before hitting the rocks and turned to look back, trying to understand what had happened. She saw the color of blood in the water a few feet away. Terrified, she tried to stay calm, praying that the shark would not come back. Swimming toward the surfer, she screamed, "Where is the other guy?"

The surfer looked at her with a puzzled face. "He's swimming in. The shark hit a seal."

She looked toward shore and saw the other surfer wading through the whitewater toward shore with his board under his arm. Her arms felt shaky and her legs tingled in the cold water beneath her, knowing there was a shark in the open ocean. She rode the next wave all the way to the beach where she was safe. The shark took off as quickly as it had appeared and did not reappear near the surfers at Trinidad Head for the rest of that day.

The great white shark swims in cold deep waters of the open ocean. White sharks can be anywhere and everywhere in temperate waters throughout the world. According to Ellis and McCosker in their book *Great White Shark*, "The white shark is a creature that lives almost wherever it chooses to, appearing and disappearing at its whim or with the seasons, usually, but not exclusively, in waters where sea lions and other pinnipeds occur." White sharks are elusive and stealthy creatures, rarely seen. Their behavior is difficult to document and many questions are not easily answered.

Sounds and signals can entice the shark when it senses activity close to the shore. Hundreds of silvery fish scatter as the shark approaches. The fish are startled by the swiftness of the shark as it appears out of nowhere, but the shark is looking for larger prey. Without ever stopping, the shark hunts for food in the waters of the Red Triangle, searching for animals resembling its prey on the surface of the water. A group of dark shapes on surfboards near the beach look like seals from below. Not a ripple reveals the shark's presence until the moment it unleashes its explosive energy.

Research shows that white sharks off the California coast travel thousands of miles, although their behavior and destinations are neither well-documented nor easy to track. Researchers have identified several sharks that live at the Farallon Islands, not far from Stinson Beach. The sharks are identified by their coloration and markings on their dorsal fins. Scientists have repeatedly spotted the same sharks in the same area.

Recent studies show that great white sharks travel farther than previously assumed. Sharks tagged at the Farallon Islands near San Francisco have traveled on long oceanic migrations to the central Pacific. Several months later, these sharks were located more than a thousand miles from the tagging site in California. Surprisingly, one shark traveled 2,280 miles from California to the Hawaiian island of Kahoolawe, near Maui, where it lingered for four months. While some sharks strayed as much as 1,000 miles, others remained close to reefs and shoals where they found a good food supply.

Great white behavior differs widely depending on location. Off California, the great whites stay mostly in the top thirty to 100 feet of water. During transit across the Pacific, they range from the surface to 2,000 feet deep.

Prior to this study, scientists believed that great whites were homebodies, sticking close to shore where their favorite prey—seals and sea lions—could easily be found. Scientists now believe that, although they are primarily coastal animals, great white sharks have both pelagic (open ocean) and deep-water phases. During their travels, great white sharks can average about forty-four miles a day, suggesting that they are strictly in transit, with little time spent feeding. Researchers now believe that white sharks may travel to Hawaii to mate and then return to the coast of California to give birth.

The study, which relied on sophisticated computers and satellite telemetry tags to record data on water depth, temperature, and light, would not have been possible even a few years earlier. The information comes at an important time, as white sharks require increased protection from international fisheries. An important step in protecting the future of sharks is to know more about them, where they go and whether they return to the same locations.

The white shark can swim long distances, covering miles of territory with ease, and can rise to the surface with incredible speed. And yet, gliding silently through the water, the shark can swim unnoticed beneath swimmers and surfers paddling or floating in the waves. Even the seals are often unaware of the shark's presence, until it strikes.

In October 2004 a neighbor who lived only a few blocks from us in Lucas Valley drove out to the coast for a day of surfing at Limantour Beach in Point Reyes National Seashore, fifty miles north of San Francisco. It was a remote stretch of beach with no other surfers in the water, but the winter swells were big and the waves were rolling in. He was floating on the waves alone in the water at about 9:30 am with his legs hanging over the sides of his board when a six- to eight-foot great white shark appeared with no warning and grabbed his leg. He felt the burning hot pain and clearly saw the shark holding onto his leg. He punched the shark on the head with all his strength and the shark let him go. He held tight to his board and fought his way through the surf back to shore, bleeding and alone at the beach. He found his cell phone in his backpack and called for a helicopter.

Park officials quickly closed the waters off Limantour Beach and adjoining Drakes Beach. A park official said the shark attack was unusual for the Point Reyes area. "I've never heard of an attack in Drakes Bay before," he said. An abalone diver was attacked at the nearby mouth of Tomales Bay in 1996 and survived his injuries. Officials noted that sea lions, elephant seals, harbor seals, as well as white sharks, frequently visit the area in the fall.

A great white shark attack is sudden, violent, fast, and unexpected. This behavior, known as ambush predation, gives the shark the benefit of surprise. The great white shark attacks its prey on the surface. At the moment of attack, the shark soars upward from below in a tremendous burst of speed and power. Even the dorsal fin may not break the surface of the water as the shark accelerates upward. The shark doesn't waste its energy until the moment of the attack, when it explodes to the surface in a burst of power. Most victims never see it coming.

It inflicts a massively destructive first bite with the intent to mortally wound its victim. Guided by instinct and superior senses, the white shark rarely attacks a victim unless it can prevail. Not wanting to risk injury to itself in an extended battle, the shark overpowers its victim with the first bite, then retreats to wait for its victim to weaken before circling back to consume the incapacitated prey. In most great white attacks, if the victim can survive the first bite and find medical attention, the victim will survive.

Other types of sharks, such as the bull shark and the tiger shark, also life threatening to humans, are more likely to make repeated attacks, and return more quickly after each bite, often until they get something. Both bull sharks and tiger sharks are known to remove limbs. Surfer Bethany Hamilton became an international sensation when she lost her arm and nearly lost her life to a fourteen-foot tiger shark while surfing the north shore of Kauai in 2003. An eight-year-old boy lost an arm to a seven-foot bull shark when he was attacked while swimming in shallow water off the coast of Florida in 2001. They boy's uncle managed to wrestle the shark to shore where he was able to retrieve the arm from its jaws. Miraculously, doctors working through the night were able to reattach the arm.

The tiger shark is second on the list of number of recorded attacks on humans, with the great white being first. Tiger sharks are found mainly in tropical and subtropical habitats, often close to the coast. They are considered by some scientists to be a near-threatened species due to finning and over-fishing by humans.

In 2003, at age thirteen, Bethany Hamilton survived a tiger shark attack on the island of Kauai that left her left arm severed. She was lying on her surfboard at 7:30 am waiting for a wave when a fourteen-foot tiger shark attacked her, ripping off her arm below the shoulder. Despite the trauma, she returned to surfing again and has become a role model for many with her faith and determination to face life's challenges.

Bull sharks can live in both saltwater and fresh water and are responsible for the majority of near-shore attacks on humans in areas other than California. They live in coastal areas of warm oceans around the world, in rivers and lakes. They can tolerate the murky water of estuaries and bays where visibility is often limited. In the United States they are seen along the coasts of Massachusetts, Florida, and Texas. Bull sharks are particularly dangerous to humans because they live in shallow water and are known for their unpredictable, often aggressive behavior. These sharks are extremely territorial and will attack other animals that enter their territory.

In July 2011 a twelve-year-old boy lost his foot but recovered from his injuries when a bull shark attacked him in less than four feet of water while he was swimming in the surf near a sand bar, off a remote beach on the Texas Gulf Coast. Humans are not part of the bull shark's normal prey, but in many cases the bull shark is simply swimming along minding its own business when it sees a fleshy object and decides to investigate or mistakes the object for food. Bull sharks can inflict extremely serious wounds.

The great white shark is capable of overpowering very large animals in violent attacks. It is the only shark that regularly feeds on warm-blooded animals. Seals and sea lions are its primary food. Like other predators, the white shark looks for easy prey, a victim that is smaller or alone, one that's apart from the others.

Shark experts have described the white shark as a picky predator. It's the largest flesh-eating shark on the planet and the most dangerous shark to humans. But great white sharks do not search out humans nor do they like the taste of humans. Rather, they mistake humans for the food they prefer, seals and sea lions.

Surfers, body boarders, and divers in wetsuits resemble seals on the surface of the water. Even swimmers in the ocean can become the target of a mistaken shark. Scientists believe this mistaken identity is a primary reason why great white sharks attack surfers, kayakers, and swimmers. The white shark attacks its prey from below. Looking up at the surface of the water, the shark sees a dark silhouette with the size and shape of a seal against the sunlit water above. The belief that sharks have poor vision is not true. Scientists believe sharks see better than humans, especially in the dim light of the ocean.

Speculation surrounds whether brighter colors might deter sharks from attacking a human, or whether sharks can even see colors. Researchers at the California Academy of Sciences in San Francisco have discovered that while great white sharks can see colors, they do not appear to use that information to discriminate in what they eat, because they generally look skyward before they attack and observe only the surface silhouette of the victim.

When a shark bites a person instead of a seal, the shark realizes the bony human is not the seal it hoped to find, and it may not return after the initial bite. Scientists refer to this as "bite and spit" behavior. The sudden and violent bite and release has been verified on large seals and sea lions by researchers at the Farallon Islands. Scientists interpret the bite and spit behavior to be adaptive because it reduces the risk of injury to the shark's sensitive eyes from the sharp teeth and nails of a struggling seal or sea lion. Sometimes the victim escapes before the shark comes back; sometimes the initial bite can be fatal.

Another theory of white shark attacks is one of investigation. Researchers towing various objects behind a small boat at the Farallon Islands report that sharks will examine almost any floating object, first cruising by for a visual inspection then, if the initial swim-by does not elicit a response from the object, the sharks frequently mouth or bite at it. This exploratory behavior suggests that white sharks may be motivated by something approximating sheer curiosity and will investigate with their mouths.

The jaws and teeth of the great white shark allow it to consume very large prey. The huge jaws unhinge to an extraordinary size, seemingly beyond proportion, with the shark's body almost dwarfed by the tremendous size and power of the jaws. Its huge mouth is lined with rows of broad, razor-sharp teeth designed for slicing chunks of flesh from seals and other large animals. Whenever a tooth is lost, a new tooth moves forward to replace it. The teeth can slice and rip the flesh of its victim, often fatally wounding its prey in a single bite. The teeth are extremely sharp, finely serrated, triangular, and nearly symmetrical. Each tooth may be as large as seven-and-a-half-centimeter (three inches) in length, row behind row. The teeth of the upper and lower jaws interlock, allowing the lower teeth to pin the prey, while the upper teeth sever the flesh like a saw blade.

A surfer was sitting on his board in the water near Half Moon Bay, south of San Francisco, waiting for a wave about 200 meters from shore. Suddenly he noticed something below the surface of the water that seemed to stop his board from moving. Looking down, he saw the head and eye of a huge shark that grasped his surfboard in its jaws. The surfer released his hold on the board, causing the protruding teeth of the upper jaw to strike his hand. He watched as the shark released its grip and swam beneath his board, disappearing into the deep water. He shouted to his friend, then grabbed his board, and rode it in to shore. The shark was not seen again and the surfer was treated for the wounds to his hand but fortunately he did not sustain permanent damage.

His surfboard with two white shark teeth embedded in it was placed on display at the Santa Cruz Surfing Museum. The size and spacing of the teeth marks in his board indicated that the shark was at least fifteen feet in length. The two teeth embedded in the board confirmed that the attacker was a great white shark and demonstrated the power of the shark's jaws.

The color of the great white shark is not completely white. Only on its underside is the white shark white. The shark is dark gray above, almost a gunmetal blue, and pale or white underneath. It is perfectly camouflaged from above and below. The counter shading, dark on top and white underneath, allows the shark to blend into its environment and surprise its prey. The shark is almost impossible to see from above with its dark back hidden against the backdrop of the ocean floor. The muscular black body glides through the ocean in dark shadowy water, nearly invisible from above. Looking up from below, the shark is pale and indistinguishable from its surroundings against the surface backlit with daylight. Perfectly camouflaged, the great white shark lives up to its well-earned reputation as a superior predator.

White sharks are also legendary because of their keen sense of smell. The white shark's acute sense of smell, combined with its ability to detect minute electrical discharges, and its sensitive inner ears, make it a predator of amazing efficiency. On the underside of its nose are two nostrils that give the white shark its sense of smell. The sharp sense of smell increases its ability to detect chemical odors and to sense the presence of other animals in the water.

The shark's nostrils have no respiratory function. Sharks are fish, and they breathe through gills. The white shark breathes through five large gills on each side of its body, just behind its head. The long, vertical gills move as the water flows through them. The white shark stays alive only by constantly moving forward and flushing oxygen-rich water over it gills. Sharks do not come to the surface to breathe air, which makes them more difficult to observe and study.

The outer skin of the white shark is covered with fine "dermal denticles," tooth-like prickles that cover the shark from the tip of its nose to its tail. The skin improves the shark's fluid dynamics so the shark can move faster. When viewed under a microscope, the skin has the appearance of pointed ridges, like a smaller version of the covering of a horseshoe crab. They also protect the shark from microscopic parasites as well as larger predators. The skin of the shark feels almost smooth when stroked from nose to tail, but the rough, sandpapery texture is unmistakable when the skin is felt from tail to nose. This is exactly the sensation I experienced when the shark bumped my hand before it attacked me.

The great white shark prowls the coastline, roaming the water in search of prey. When the shark senses activity close to shore, its eyes and sensory receptors lead it to the beach where black shapes paddle together on the surface like a seal colony. The great white shark glides with tremendous speed and power, perfectly designed for agility and graceful movements.

Scientists with Scripps Institute of Oceanography have shown that a white shark can find its prey even in the dark, and even when the prey is buried in the sand. Sharks are believed to use this sensitivity not only to detect their prey, but also to navigate and orient themselves with respect to earth's magnetic field and to electrical signals generated by ocean currents, which are detected by the shark.

The hunting expertise of the great white shark, described by Ellis and McCosker, employs "a battery of sensory devices that might rival the detection systems of nuclear submarines." It is a skilled hunter preying chiefly upon seals, sea lions, fish, squid, and whales.

As the white shark nears a seal, swimmer, or surfer, it can detect turbulence and vibrations created by movement in the water. Through a system of sensory cells embedded in the skin, it can sense water currents and pressure changes caused by an animal in the water. Movement in the water displaces the sensory-cell hairs in the shark's network of pressure-wave detectors.

In September 1998, a month after my attack, a young man paddling a yellow kayak moved silently and smoothly across the surface of the water, following the coastline near Bolinas in the morning fog. His wide paddle splashed and slapped the waves as he pulled it across the surface with each stroke, sending ripples through the water. The rhythm of the paddle sent signals of sound and energy to a shark, causing its keen senses to zero in on the activity that came from this shape on the surface.

The young man felt something solid bump his kayak as he moved. The glancing blow rocked the unsteady boat. Frightened, the man looked straight down into the water but saw nothing but shadows. He didn't think a shark could check him out and disappear so quickly. However, his small boat resembled the shape of a seal from the water below and he'd become the target of a shark. The shape and sound of the kayak were picked up by the shark's keen senses. Suddenly the shark approached the kayak, its wide jaws open, and tried to engulf the shape that resembled a seal. The touch and smell of plastic were not what the shark expected. The shark lost interest and quickly retreated, forced to continue hunting for food. The man regained his balance on the water and turned his kayak, paddling furiously toward shore, hoping the shark was gone.

White sharks also have a system of gel-filled pores called the ampullae of Lorenzini, used to detect electrical impulses. Capsules beneath the skin sense minute electrical discharges through a system of sensory cells embedded in the skin, interconnected by a fluid-filled canal. Sea animals and swimmers produce an electrical current where their skin meets the water, and from the membranes of their mouth or gills. The more rapidly the gills beat or the muscles move, the greater the current the shark is able to detect. The muscles of a frightened swimmer kicking hard can send an even more powerful signal, easily picked up by the shark.

The white shark can sense even extremely faint electrical currents generated by living creatures, giving it the ability to detect the presence of prey underwater. It can detect electrical impulses given off by the beating heart, gill action, or muscles of another animal, its prey. Sharks are believed to use this sensitivity not only to detect prey, but also to navigate and orient themselves with respect to the earth's magnetic field and currents of the ocean moving through it, creating electrical signals that are detected by the shark.

When an animal is flailing or splashing, the muscles give off electrical currents the shark can sense. These signals attract the shark to its prey. The muscles of a swimmer kicking hard, trying to get away, emit electrical impulses. The shark can zero in on the source of the signals and attack precisely at that point.

The day I was attacked at Stinson Beach in August 1998, after the shark bumped my hand, my kicking hard to get away would have increased the intensity of signals from the muscles in my legs and created a disturbance the shark could not ignore. The shark's sensitive detectors received the signals of my presence and did not fail to notice that I was alone and one of the smallest. The shark zeroed in on me and accelerated to the surface in a blazing burst of energy.

Año Nuevo State Reserve, fifty-five miles south of San Francisco, is a rocky point that juts into the Pacific, and home of the largest mainland breeding colony for northern elephant seals. Researchers at Año Nuevo have tagged great white sharks with sub-sonic tracking devices with a signature beacon. The tracking will reveal information about the behavior of the sharks that live in and around the Red Triangle and will increase our knowledge and awareness about sharks.

In September 2008 Stinson Beach reopened to swimmers and surfers after being closed for more than a week following two sightings of great white sharks. Lifeguards closed the beach after a fisherman and lifeguard reported a ten-foot great white shark seventy-five yards from shore. The closure was extended after a second sighting in the same place a few days later. News reports said the beach reopened "amid great white shark fears."

"It's been a bad year for sharks, with shark sightings up and down the west coast putting beachgoers on edge." The ABC news report followed numerous sightings and a shark attack on a surfer 150 yards from shore at Marina Beach along the central coast of California near Santa Barbara. His friends heard him yelling "Shark," and after helping him to shore, they used towels as tourniquets to stop the bleeding in his arm and neck. He was airlifted to a nearby hospital and expected to make a full recovery.

A US Coast Guard crew in a helicopter spotted an eight-to ten-foot shark 200 yards offshore from Stinson Beach. The National Park Service immediately ordered swimmers out of the water. Witnesses at the beach said the reaction by swimmers was immediate and the water was empty within five minutes; but no one on shore or in the water saw the shark. One lifeguard observed, "Sharks are out there on a regular basis. Whether or not they are sighted is happenstance. We know this is where the sharks are."

In December 2006, a twelve- to fifteen-foot great white shark attacked a surfer at Dillon Beach north of Stinson Beach, in Marin County, California. The surfer, resting on his board waiting for a wave about seventy yards off the beach, felt a surge of water beneath him. A great white shark slammed into him suddenly from below, lifting him out of the water and clamping onto his surfboard with its teeth penetrating through his board. The surfer held onto his board with all his might as the shark dragged him fifteen feet underwater. Finally, with the resistance of the board, the shark released him and he rocketed up out of the water. He suffered bites to his hip and torso, with teeth marks penetrating his board. The surfer was lucky to survive.

Authorities posted signs warning swimmers and surfers at the beach that sightings of great white sharks are fairly common in these waters. A state beach ranger said, "We post warning signs, but people can enter at their own risk. People who use the water out here know you are entering into another food chain."

On an October morning in 1996, at 9:30 am, beautiful waves were rolling in along the North Coast. There was a crowd in the water near Dillon Beach at the north end of Tomales Bay, thirty-six miles north of Stinson Beach. Suddenly, without warning, a shark struck a twenty-two-year-old who was surfing only fifteen yards from shore, completely grabbing his leg and his board and pulling him under the water. He looked the shark in the eye, later saying it was "like looking into the eye of the living dead." Nearby surfers described a fifteen- to eighteen-foot shark with unbelievable power and a huge fin that rose three feet out of the water. It bit completely through his kneecap.

The surfer's father described the big shark as it swam away, "When it swam off, its wake was like a submarine." The shark quickly disappeared and other surfers in the water helped the victim to shore. "It was a very long paddle because we knew the thing was still out there somewhere. This is one nightmare you think can never happen to you."

"I feel lucky; I could be dead," the injured surfer said.

In August 1996 a shark attacked an abalone diver near Tomales Point not far away. The diver, who received fifty stitches, was bitten twice and was fortunate to survive. A park ranger noted that "more sharks could be expected in the coming months" as they follow the elephant seals that come to the area to breed.

In December 1996 a surfer at Dillon Beach saw the jaws of a twelve- to fifteen- foot great white shark clamp down on his board, its teeth slicing through his board. The surfer received superficial wounds but escaped major injury. The shark dragged him fifteen feet under water and he was held down for so long he thought he would drown. The surfer reported this was his fourth brush with a shark—three times a shark had bumped him while surfing and once, four years earlier, he had helped his friend who was attacked at Bodega Bay. This time, he said he was "going to hang it up."

In October 2010, a nineteen-year-old surfer was not as fortunate when he was attacked at Surf Beach near Santa Barbara. He suffered the loss of his leg, resulting in massive blood loss. It happened so quickly his friends were not able to get him to shore in time, and they were not able to save his life. Authorities believed the shark was a great white, between seventeen and eighteen feet long, weighing approximately 4,000 pounds.

It was mid-afternoon May 31, 2002 in the Red Triangle just off the coast of Bolinas, two miles from Stinson Beach. The twelve- to fourteen-foot great white shark hit the twenty-four-year-old surfer with unexpected force about 300 yards offshore, throwing him into the air, striking the left side of his body, biting from his ribs down to his thigh, and clenching him in its jaws. Fellow surfers nearby heard screams and saw the razor sharp jaws clench down to his bone as the shark lifted him three feet out of the water. The surfers said they could see the shark's teeth and gums, its closed eyes, and its gills wide open "like shutters." The shark's dorsal fin and back were completely out of the water. The shark crashed back into the ocean suddenly releasing the surfer. The other surfers circled around to protect him and help him back to shore. He was loaded into a helicopter and flown to a local hospital where the trauma surgeon said he was in critical condition but the injuries were not life threatening. When asked what it looked like, the surfer said, "It was a large white shark with large white teeth."

The Pacific water along the coast of Northern California offers a rich bounty of marine life and an abundant food supply. Sharks follow the food supply that moves with the seasons and currents. In late August and September, the sharks feed closer to shore where the nutrients are plentiful.

Dusty Payne, a pro surfer from Hawaii participating in the November 2011 Rip Curl Pro Search surf competition, made a sudden exit from the water after seeing a large and menacing shark just outside the lineup during competition at Ocean Beach in San Francisco. Lifeguards patrolled the water by boat and saw nothing. The next heat of the competition continued but the shark sighting had a chilling effect on the competition for the rest of the day. "I've seen dolphins," Payne said, "and it wasn't a dolphin."

The shark sighting didn't deter local surfer Nate McCarthy, who showed up to compete in the Expression Session of the Rip Curl competition. Nate was running late and, with fifteen surfers already in the water, he had just enough time to throw on his wetsuit and paddle out to the lineup. He was in the right spot to catch a nice left and show off with a couple of good turns, rocketing all the way to the finish line to capture first place. His victory brought him a prize of $1,000 as well as some well-earned recognition for his Mill Valley surf shop called "Proof Lab," a favorite stop for Bay Area surfers on the way to the beach. The pro surfers from Hawaii might be afraid of a shark swimming near the lineup, but it seemed to be no big deal for the locals who know the sharks are out there.

Scientists believe that most attacks on humans are accidents and the great white shark does not deserve its fearsome reputation. Within a few seconds the great white can determine whether its prey is a rich source of food, sufficient to justify the attack. The shark does not want to expend its energy for a meal that is not worthwhile. This may explain why, in some cases, the shark bites a human and then turns away. The shark quickly determines that the person is not what it wants to eat. The shark recognizes that human flesh is not the same as the fat-laden outer layer of a seal or sea lion. The fat making up the insulating coat of seals has more energy content than human muscle. The white shark has an amazing ability to discern whether something it bites is low in nutritional value in comparison to seals and sea lions.

"Your Brain on Nature" was the cover story for the December 2011 issue of *Outside* magazine. The article describes fascinating theories and current discoveries by researcher and marine biologist Wallace J. Nichols about why we love the ocean. Nichols observes people at the ocean and in front of the coral reef tank at the California Academy of Science. The tank holds 212,000 gallons of water with huge windows displaying colorful fish, corals, and sea creatures. He notices how people grow quiet and calm, couples hold hands, and wonderful things happen in the presence of the great blue space of water. Nichols says people become more centered, more serene, and happier in the presence of the huge tank resembling the ocean.

Studies show nature has many positive effects on our minds, improving attention span, memory, and mood as well as reducing stress. Nichols and other cognitive researchers are investigating what being in nature does to our brains. Research shows meditation can ease anxiety after an emotional event; similar processes might be going on in the brains of surfers who react immediately to a rising wave and then enjoy the time between the waves.

Something happens to us at the ocean. Gazing out over the ocean can slow your breathing. Your mind and body relax. You experience joy. Surfing or even looking out over the ocean can calm and renew us. This phenomenon offers hope for saving the oceans.

Nichols is convinced that our love of the ocean will become a powerful new tool to protect oceans. He's confident that neurological research will further his neuro-conservation drive. He speaks to audiences with a message of hope. He believes our love for the oceans will help us save the oceans. Our fondness for the great blue world may indeed be the one thing that will save the oceans.

Great white sharks have been wrongly portrayed in popular culture ever since Peter Benchley published his novel *Jaws* about the shark attack at a fictional town called Amity. His story of the shark made readers wonder if it would ever be safe to go into the water again. Movies, myths, and sensational media have contributed to this reputation of the great white shark as a killer. Stories and menacing pictures have exaggerated the white shark's threat to humans.

We now know that sharks are essential and important members of the fascinating world of the ocean. Fortunately, public awareness is increasing and we are beginning to understand the shark's surprising vulnerability and appreciate its valuable role in our environment. We are learning that sharks are critical for healthy oceans.

CAN WE SAVE THE GREAT WHITE SHARK?

"After a thousand years of darkness, we may be seeing the first inklings of a healthy concern for this unreasonably maligned and misunderstood creature."
—Dr. John McCosker, Shark Expert

In the few years since my attack, changes have taken place in our understanding of sharks and the ocean. Scientists recognize sharks as apex predators, critical to maintaining the balance of the ocean environment. White sharks help to limit the populations of their prey. Because their diets vary, they can switch preferred species when certain populations are low, allowing a species to persist. By preventing one species from dominating limited resources, these top predators increase the species diversity of the ecosystem. Without sharks to control the numbers of seals and fish, populations become out of balance and can quickly boom and then decline when their food supply runs out. As superior predators, sharks help maintain the ocean by culling populations of the old, the weak, or the sick.

The ocean is a living environment increasingly endangered by human activities such as overfishing, pollution, and shark finning—activities which also impact sharks. Although white sharks are protected in the waters of California, the white shark's existence worldwide is in danger. Scientists believe that one-third of open-ocean sharks are now threatened with extinction with some shark populations experiencing a ninety-nine percent decline. Some believe the great white shark is on its way to becoming an endangered species.

When we kill sharks we not only imperil the shark population but also a vast array of other species in the ocean, many yet unknown to us. In some places the ocean is nearly seven miles deep and we have only begun to explore its depths and the creatures that live there.

Oceans cover seventy-one percent of the earth, supporting vast life forms. The great oceans, the Atlantic, Pacific, Indian, and Arctic, hold ninety-eight percent of our planet's water and an estimated eighty percent of the world's biodiversity. There are at least 30,000 kinds of fish, more than any other vertebrate on earth. Healthy oceans depend on sharks and yet no one knows how many great white sharks there are in the world. By studying sharks we hope to find clues to the environment and why some species are disappearing.

As top predators in the marine ecosystem, sharks are naturally scarce. While some fish may produce thousands or even millions of eggs each year, many shark species reproduce much more slowly. Sharks may take twenty or more years to reach maturity. For millions of years large sharks had few natural predators and this survival strategy served them well. But years of overfishing and exploitation by humans have made their recovery slow and difficult.

In April 2012, two Mexican fishermen hauling up their net in the Sea of Cortez thought they had a large catch of small fish but were surprised to find a large great white shark measuring 20 feet in length and 2,000 pounds. Unfortunately the shark was dead because these sharks live only by moving constantly and flushing water over their gills. This incident is simply an example of threats to the white shark population due to accidental by-catch. It is particularly unfortunate when a species is so large and slow growing.

For years, sharks have been killed for their fins. Scientists believe this practice is pushing some shark species to the brink of extinction. The fins are used in shark fin soup, a traditional delicacy in some cultures. The shark fin itself has no taste, only texture, but shark fin soup is a symbol of status in many Asian cultures.

Shark finning is a cruel and wasteful practice that involves pulling the shark into the boat, cutting off the fins, and throwing the shark back into the ocean to die. These sharks thrown back into the ocean bleed to death or drown because sharks cannot swim without fins and they need to move forward to get oxygen.

Awareness of shark finning has resulted in recent legislation to ban the trade, possession, or sale of shark fins in California, Washington, Oregon, Hawaii, and Guam. The swell of worldwide opposition has grown and in January 2012, just days before the Lunar New Year, the luxury Shangri-La hotel chain announced it would ban shark fin soup from all of its seventy-two hotels, mostly located in

Asia. According to WildAid, about ninety-five percent of all shark fin soup is consumed in China although there are markets in Japan, Hong Kong, Singapore, Korea, and even in the US.

The trend to stop this practice is growing but further education is needed. Conservation groups like Sea Stewards and WildAid, along with scientists around the world, are working to prohibit shark finning and the sale of shark fins. These new laws are making shark fins much like ivory—illegal to own or sell.

If sharks wanted to eat us, they could; but they don't. Most days, surfers are spread out and vulnerable in the water. If sharks wanted an easy snack, they could chase down a person, but they rarely do. When they do, it's most likely because they mistake a person for a seal and most people survive. White sharks can easily devour larger prey, but they quickly recognize that people are not what they want to eat. The fact that pigs eat more people than sharks may not be comforting when you are in the jaws of the great white shark.

However great the number of shark attacks on people, sharks have much more to fear from us than we have from them. Humans kill millions of sharks each year. Many are "by-catch," snagged by fishermen targeting other species on long lines or trawl nets. Others are killed for thriving markets in shark products such as shark fins, skin, oil, and cartilage used in some cultures as food, beauty, and folk treatments. Even its superior abilities cannot protect the white shark from the greatest predator of all time—humans.

Great white sharks are victims of misperception and media hype, often portrayed as villains. Sharks stir terror in our souls. And yet, of the hundreds of species of sharks, only a few species are dangerous to humans.

After publication of his book, *Jaws*, Peter Benchley realized the damage he'd done to the reputation of the great white shark. He saw the effects his books and movies had on people's fear and willingness to brutally slaughter any kind of shark—large or small. He dedicated the remaining years of his life to shark protection, saying, "The predator is now the prey, the villain is now the victim."

My support for sharks may seem surprising, but after my attack I talked to many shark experts and learned more about the beauty and importance of the great white shark. I began to collaborate with the nonprofit groups WildAid and Sea Stewards, participating in events to protect sharks.

Working with WildAid to help educate people about sharks
on Shark Day at the Cal Academy in San Francisco

With Peter Benchley, author of Jaws *and* Shark Trouble, *at a Shark Day fundraiser for WildAid*

With David McGuire speaking at "Sharktober," an event to save sharks, in San Francisco

Book release party for our book, Far from Shore

In 2002, I was fortunate to have an opportunity to appear with Peter Benchley at "Shark Day" to promote shark awareness and shark education at the California Academy of Sciences in San Francisco. Mr. Benchley met my family and signed his new book, *Shark Trouble,* for us. We talked about how sharks need our help to improve their image.

I studied sharks and ocean biology while I was a student at UC Berkeley and lectured as a guest speaker for ocean geography. I began my lecture with information and statistics about shark attacks along the California coast.

Filming a National Geographic documentary
at Cronkite Beach north of San Francisco

Speaking at a shark event in San Francisco

The students looked detached from any real connection to the subject until I told them I was one of these victims. Suddenly the students became more interested in hearing my real-life experience. I began to realize how my personal story could provide a lead-in to capture the interest of my audience. Whenever I make a presentation on behalf of saving sharks and the oceans, I use my story and to increase awareness and encourage others to become involved in saving sharks.

I've learned to appreciate the beauty of sharks and their importance in the ocean environment. I encourage people to save sharks, even the one that attacked me. I've been involved in events to stop shark finning, working with the San Francisco Sea Stewards to promote healthy oceans. Despite being attacked by a shark, I believe sharks are a vital part of our ecosystem and should be protected. I encourage others to respect the shark's right to live in the ocean.

Oceans are wilderness places, mostly still unexplored and filled with an amazing abundance of life. Henry Thoreau appreciated the simplicity of the outdoors and the unmatchable qualities of nature. His words describe the wild beauty we need to preserve: "In wildness is the preservation of the world."

When I look at the ocean, I see a world that deserves our protection, respect, and awe. The ocean is a place that enchants us and sustains us, a world we need to protect for generations to come. I was swimming in the shark's world that day; the shark belongs there and I was the visitor. In the ocean, there are no boundaries; the shark does not know about beaches. When we're in the ocean, we're in the shark's world.

AFTERWORD

Think of the Shark

Wallace J. Nichols, PhD
Research Associate, California Academy of Sciences
Found of BLUEMIND: The Mind and Ocean Initiative

If you've been paying attention all these years you know that like a conveyor belt a shark can continuously replace lost teeth over and over again. A shark's body is covered with dermal "teeth" that give it hydrodynamic advantages. Pores connected to nerves act as a sixth sense and read electrical signals from prey. A shark's jaws aren't attached to its cranium. You might say that it is supremely efficient for hunting and eating from nose to tail, from skin to skeleton.

Now, feel the shark.

Not with your fingers, but with your entire, complex and exquisite nervous system.

Put aside what you think you know—and really feel the shark.

From deep in your amygdala, the seat of primitive emotions, to the tips of your toes a shark feels like a shiver.

Bathed in dopamine, your brain on shark is rewarded with precisely what it has always craved. Addiction isn't too strong a word. In fact, it's precisely the correct word.

If you pull the electric threads that make up each wave in that shiver you'll discover awe, lust, fear, longing, strength, hunger, jealousy and that you are right at home.

Feel the shark.

It's said that you remember most and understand best when you feel. So, feel.

With a flash from its black eye, the cut of its dorsal fin or the flick of its tail, the shark demands that you feel. There's nothing polite about it. It all happens so quickly.

Meanwhile, the front of your brain works to make sense of shark memories, films, stories, prose, information and context.

Together your modern and ancient mind simultaneously asks every neuron in your body the same question: What are you going to do now?

How you respond to that question will determine your future. It will decide the fate of sharks. And it will foreshadow what our planet's single greatest feature, the ocean, becomes.

Does your body-mind tell you to live? Yes it does.

You can never comprehend the ocean until you feel the shark. You'll never fully feel the shark until you know your own mind. And you have just scratched the surface. Congratulations.

Feel the shark.

Know yourself.

Comprehend the ocean.

Love.

HOW TO AVOID
A SHARK ATTACK

A few reminders:

- Never swim or surf alone. If you're in the ocean, you're in the shark's territory.
- Avoid places with lots of seals. You could be a victim of mistaken identity.
- Avoid the mouths of rivers and places where people have been attacked by sharks.
- Don't go out beyond everyone else where you'll be the easiest target and far from assistance.
- Stay inside the seals. If a seal swims to shore, something might be chasing it.
- Stay out of the water in Northern California during "shark season," from August through October.
- Don't swim or surf near fishing boats, especially if birds are diving for food in the water.
- Use a larger surfboard to create the image of a larger, less vulnerable prey.
- Be alert to subtle cues or activity in your environment telling you something's not right.
- If a shark attacks, fight back. Keep trying. Do whatever it takes. Never, ever give up.

OCEAN CONSERVATION RESOURCES:

For Further Information and Ways to Make a Difference

MarineBio
www.marinebio.org/oceans/conservation/organizations_issue.asp

Monterey Bay Aquarium
www.montereybayaquarium.org

The California Academy of Sciences
www.calacademy.org

The Nature Conservancy
www.nature.org

Sea Stewards
www.seastewards.org

Environmental Defense
www.edf.org

The Oceanic Society
www.oceanicsociety.org

Oceana
www.oceana.org

WildAid
www.wildaid.org

Save Our Shores
www.saveourshores.org

ABOUT THE AUTHORS

Jonathan Kathrein is a graduate of University of California Berkeley, winner of the San Francisco Chronicle Jefferson Award for Service to the Community, and author of *Don't Fear the Shark*, a children's story that is a metaphor for treating others well. (www.dontfeartheshark.com.) Jonathan is the co-founder of the nonprofit Future Leaders For Peace, now E 3. He is a motivational and public speaking coach. He has appeared on many radio and TV programs, including *Dateline NBC*, the Discovery Channel, *How to Survive*, *Travel Emergencies*, *Fox Mornings on Two*, *View from the Bay*, National Geographic's *Shark Battleground*—The Red Triangle, and *People of the Year* in Germany. He has lectured to classes at UC Berkeley. His interviews have appeared in *Surfer Magazine*, *BodyBoarding*, the *San Francisco Chronicle*, *Sports Illustrated*, and more. Jonathan's interview for "Primal Scream" was the headline program for The Discovery Channel's "Shark Week." He is the co-author of *Far From Shore: A Mother's Memoir of a Shark Attack*. Jonathan continues his efforts to protect our environment and is currently working with Ygrene Energy, a company dedicated to sustainable energy. The author lives with his wife, Ashlee, and their daughter in Mill Valley,

Margaret Kathrein is a graduate of Marquette University and Loyola University Law School. She is the mother of three sons, Jonathan, Michael, and Eric. She is a former flight attendant for Pan American World Airways, and a former associate with the Chicago law firm of Burditt and Radzius specializing in food and drug law. With her son Jonathan, she is the co-author of *Far From Shore: A Mother's Memoir of a Shark Attack* (www.FarFromShoreTheBook.com). She has also written *Crisis Management,* and she is co-author of *Occupational Health Law.* She has appeared with Jonathan on *View From the Bay,* as well as other television and radio programs. The author and her husband, Reed, reside in Lucas Valley, Marin County, in the San Francisco Bay Area.

Books by the same authors:

Don't Fear the Shark
By Jonathan Kathrein
www.DontFeartheShark.com

Far From Shore, A Mother's Memoir of a Shark Attack
By Margaret Kathrein and Jonathan Kathrein
www.FarFromShoreTheBook.com